STEWART FORD

THE INSIDE STORY OF A NEW GRAND PRIX TEAM'S RACE TO THE FORMULA 1 GRID

"My toughest challenge," by Jackie Stewart

Two legends

FORD: FIGHTING BACK TO THE FRONT   STEWART'S WINNING WAYS

one dream

MEET THE DRIVERS • INSIDE THE STEWART-FORD PIT • FIRING UP THE V10

I f anyone harboured doubts about Ford's commitment to the sport of grand prix racing, events in 1996 must certainly have reassured them. In January came confirmation of the Blue Oval's revolutionary new partnership with Jackie and Paul Stewart. And by December – just 11 months later! – the first tartan-bedecked SF-1 was running in anger, guided by the experienced hands of grand prix stalwart Rubens Barrichello.

To have built not just a state-of-the-art Formula One car but an entire grand prix team in this time is a minor miracle. Of course, it would take something more than that to see Rubens or his team-mate, Jan Magnussen, celebrating Stewart-Ford's first victory in 1997. But make no mistake, this is a team filled with proven winners, and they mean to win again.

We hope the next 30-odd pages make it possible for you to follow the team's progress with even greater interest. For Stewart-Ford, the battle has only just begun.

STEVE CROPLEY
Editor-in-chief, AUTOCAR

Editor Mike Herd Designer Frances Kiernan Written by Simon Taylor, Alan Henry, Colin Goodwin Photography Darren Heath (unless credited) Assistant editor Peter McSean Production Stuart White International editions GERMANY Nicolaus Koretzky, Dr Karen Eriksen, Christel Flexney, Matthias Penzel FRANCE Jean-Michel Desnoues BRAZIL Lito Cavalcanti, Flavio Gomez, Leonardo Rocha Publishing director Simon Daukes Editor-in-chief Steve Cropley Thanks to Louise Teesdale & Stephen Wright

Repro: Fairway Litho, 3-4 Seax Way, Basildon, Essex. (01268) 541 234.
Printers: CSM Impact, Impact House, Units 1-2 Grafton Way, West Ham Industrial Estate, Basingstoke, Hants. (01256) 479 816. Published by Haymarket Magazines Ltd, 38–42 Hampton Road, Teddington, Middlesex TW11 0JE. © Haymarket Magazines Ltd 1997
REPRINTING IN WHOLE OR PART IS FORBIDDEN EXCEPT BY PERMISSIONS. THE PUBLISHERS MAKE EVERY EFFORT TO ENSURE THIS SUPPLEMENT'S CONTENTS ARE CORRECT, AND CANNOT ACCEPT RESPONSIBILITY FOR ANY ERRORS OR OMISSIONS

London, 10 December: amid hordes of international press, the first Stewart-Ford SF-1 is launched

DARREN HEATH

Contents
STEWART-FORD SUPPLEMENT

4 THE RACER'S EDGE
Behind the new Stewart-Ford challenge is one of Formula One's most memorable success stories

6 FAMILY BUSINESS
Chairman and triple world champion admits: "This is the toughest test of my life"

To most mortals, clinching a third world title would be the pinnacle of a dream Formula One career. To Jackie Stewart, it was only the beginning....

THE
racer's
edge

BY SIMON TAYLOR

Once a racer, always a racer. Jackie Stewart can't remember exactly when the idea of running his own grand prix team took root. But he's sure it's going to be the biggest challenge of his life.

Telling words from a man who has written his name indelibly into the history books as one of motor racing's all-time greats. A man who started 99 grands prix, won 27 of them, and was world champion three times in five years.

He arrived in Formula One in 1965 as a bouncy, cheeky young Scot, team-mate to the more patrician Graham Hill at BRM. Illness as a child, and dyslexia, meant Jackie had been a failure at school. Until he found he could reach Olympic standard at clay pigeon shooting, he'd never been much of a success at anything. Then he discovered motor racing, and immediately became a man to watch.

He scored a point in his first grand prix, and that first year went on to stand on the podium five times, winning the Italian Grand Prix and finishing third in the championship. Then the following year, in the Belgian Grand Prix, he crashed.

He'd just won the Monaco Grand Prix and was leading the world championship. At Spa he started from the front row, and half way round the first lap the field ran into a rain storm. His BRM ended up well off the track, upside down in a field, with

Stewart trapped inside, soaked in petrol. There were no marshals to be seen and it was left to two other drivers, unhurt in their own accidents, to free the injured driver from the wreck. Almost half an hour passed before an ambulance arrived to take him to hospital.

Jackie was racing again a month later, as quick and as bouncy as ever, but suddenly he'd matured. Now he was a man with a mission: he believed it was possible to remove a lot of unnecessary risk from the sport. Thanks to the campaign that he helped to initiate, motor racing has over the years become immeasurably safer.

His efforts did not always make him popular with the establishment, but Jackie is not an easy man to stop when he has set his sights on a goal. Generations of drivers now owe their lives to his crusading zeal, which has led to today's impressive medical facilities, infinitely safer circuits, and a general understanding of how to run motor racing properly.

By 1968 two vital partnerships had begun: with Ken Tyrrell, and with the

Main picture: "One down...." Jackie celebrates his first world drivers' crown after winning the 1969 Italian GP. Left: 1971 sportsman of the year meets his female counterpart, HRH Princess Anne. Below: Fashionably long hair won public and media approval!

AUTOSPORT

Ford DFV engine. World Championships followed in 1969, 1971 and 1973. Jackie's status as Formula One's top driver lent authority to his determination to bring a new professionalism to the sport, while his fashionably long hair showed his understanding of the celebrity status he now enjoyed in the mass media. In a variety of ways, Jackie Stewart had made himself the first modern racing driver.

And when, at the age of 34, he retired from the cockpit, Stewart's racing fame became the springboard to a new career as an international businessman. Boardroom doors opened for him all over the world. His mix of canny shrewdness, easygoing charm and boundless energy earned him directorships of Ford and Goodyear, and involvements in a variety of other projects.

He was comfortable in front of a camera and with a microphone, and his image in the USA became so connected with the British way of life that an American TV network used him to cover a royal wedding. His flying miles on endless business trips around the world from his Swiss home near Geneva grew to be measured in millions. In his business career, he earned far more than he had in his nine years of Formula One.

Always there was the integrity, the relentless energy, the passionate attention to detail. If you ever got involved with a Jackie project, you found everything had to be right, no matter how long it took.

And still motor racing beckoned. Perhaps, like any fond parent, Jackie wasn't too pleased when one of his sons, Paul, decided to take it up. But, between them, they gave birth to Paul Stewart Racing, and a new chapter opened in Jackie's life. Now that has led to father and son working together to build a new Formula One team capable of competing in the toughest of racing environments. The white and blue cars with the tartan stripes may be brand new, but they have a great heritage behind them – and, crucially, the Ford relationship which began in the 1960s continues to be a central part of that heritage.

Jackie and Paul regard this season as the first stage of a long-term project. They are hungry for results, but they're also realistic about the time-frame, and are under no illusions about the magnitude of the task in this highest-tech, most competitive sport on earth. But the team has all the will, the determination, the professionalism and the talent needed to get Stewart-Ford to the very top.

For Jackie, the goal is there, and he means to hit it. Once a racer, always a racer.... ◾

Highland dynasty

PAUL STEWART RACING

It's not easy building a racing career as the son of a famous motor racing father. Damon Hill will tell you that. And when the 17-year-old Paul Stewart told his father he wanted to have a go, Jackie told him his university education had to come first.

It wasn't until 1988, when Paul was 21, that Paul Stewart Racing was founded to run a single Formula Ford car. Naturally, the approach was ultra-professional, and the team rapidly grew into the ideal base for many a young driver. As Paul's cockpit career progressed to Formula 3000 so PSR rose to prominence in numerous single-seater formulae.

The record speaks for itself: over nine years, the team has won an extraordinary 107 races and 10 championships – an unparalleled achievement. One graduate of the Stewart 'staircase of talent' was brilliant Jan Magnussen, who won 14 out of 18 British Formula 3 championship rounds in 1994 – and is now in his first full Formula One season with Stewart-Ford.

By the end of 1993, Paul had done three years in F3000 and was trying to put together a Formula One drive when he decided, abruptly, that his future lay away from the cockpit. A courageous decision, it allowed him to concentrate on developing Paul Stewart Racing, which now continues alongside the new team.

Anyone who heard Paul's emotional speech at the launch of the new car will know that the father-and-son bond is very strong. As chairman and managing director respectively, Jackie and Paul represent a remarkable motor racing dynasty. Their skills are complementary but, when results come, their joys will be the same.

Family business

"To be doing this with my son
Paul is terrific. I don't think I
could have done it without him"

Jackie Stewart tells
ALAN HENRY *that the*
Stewart-Ford team
is anything but a
one man show

LEAD PHOTO: TERRY O'NEILL

"**A** reputation is built on the past. But success is built on today and in the future, and that's what we have to deliver. We *have* to deliver. I've always needed to deliver in whatever I have undertaken, and I'll be trying awfully hard to do just that."

Nothing that triple world champion Jackie Stewart experienced during his nine seasons behind the wheel has matched the challenge which he and his son Paul faced in establishing the new Formula One team. It's been a tortuous road just to make it to the grid, but at last they have the team, the engine and the sponsorship – and now the real battle begins.

"Sometimes I find myself feeling that winning those three world championships seemed very easy by comparison. Seriously, winning world titles is never easy, but I had a fantastic team behind me with Ken Tyrrell and that helped me a lot.

"Now we have to fulfil that same role; we are those people behind the drivers. And it has certainly been a greater challenge, more complicated and more difficult than simply being a driver. I wouldn't take anything away from a Schumacher or a Hill, or any of the other current drivers, but it is easier than putting this together. I think even Alain Prost will one day say the same thing, because the complexities involved in establishing a team are *far beyond* anything that faces a driver.

"As far as the prospects for our first season in Formula One are concerned, I would expect we might be qualifying around 12th to 14th, and it would be a great achievement to score perhaps a few championship points by the end of the year. But we are very aware of the

7

Paul

GREG BARTLEY

"Paul deserves huge credit for the way he has built up the new team"

I have been enormously proud of Paul's achievements. That goes right back to the time I remember telling him that I was totally opposed to his going motor racing on his own.

He came back from the 1983 British Grand Prix and produced a brochure from the racing school at Silverstone. Unknown to me, he had signed up for the course. He wanted me to help him, and I refused, telling him I really thought he should complete his university studies before he turned his attention to anything like that.

To be honest, when I told him that, I felt really bad. Here we were, sitting outside our home, with its pool and its tennis court, all those privileges having come out of what he was wanting to do – and I was telling him that he couldn't do it!

But Paul completed his studies and eventually went motor racing. We established Paul Stewart Racing originally as a vehicle just to enter his own car, and it is largely to Paul's credit that we were celebrating the team's 100th win by the end of the 1996 season – three years after he himself retired from driving.

As for the development of the Stewart Grand Prix infrastructure, Paul deserves a huge amount of credit. He has worked diligently behind the scenes with our technical director, Alan Jenkins, and I think the merit of those efforts will soon become fully visible. I don't think I could have established the Formula One team without Paul, and I don't think I would have wanted to do it without him either....

challenge which awaits us. There are many other teams out there with vastly more experience than ourselves."

Jackie is keen to make the point that he never promised any specific results when he was behind the wheel, and it is the same with Stewart-Ford. But he also believes that the most pressure to achieve success will come from within the team itself.

"I never promised a win or a championship when I was a racing driver," he insists. "I wanted to deliver the best that I could. If it was good enough, we would win; if we were really good enough, we would win a world championship. That is what we now have to do again, but in a much more complicated environment.

"You know how critical the media can be and I don't expect any quarter! I expect to get just what everybody else gets. Inevitably, there will be supporters and detractors. But we only have to deliver for us, the Stewart-Ford team.

"We can't worry what other people are saying. We have to do it in our own time, at our own pace, building the correct foundations for success. If you force-feed a tomato, you won't get the same flavour

"I am a very proud Scot. I feel a lot for my wee country – there are only five million of us, and our greatest export has always been the people"

out of it than from one you allow to grow in its own time. We've got to be given that opportunity, and I hope too many people don't expect too much too soon."

Of course, Jackie feels an enormous amount of pride in his Scottish ancestry, as reflected by the specially designed Stewart Racing Tartan which bedecks the Stewart-Ford SF-1.

"I am a very proud Scot," Jackie says. "The whole family were born in Scotland. I feel a lot for my wee country; there are only five million of us, and our greatest export has always been the people. So I like the idea of the team's tartan identification. My racing helmet wore Royal Stewart tartan, Paul's wore Stewart Hunting tartan, and the Stewart Racing tartan is a combination of the two."

Jackie is acutely aware of his own motor racing heritage and how the opportunities he enjoyed effectively opened a path – many years later – for him and Paul to start their own grand prix team from scratch.

"When I announced my retirement from driving on 14 October, 1973, I surely could not have known what my long-term future would be," he reflects.

"You know how critical the media can be – I don't expect any quarter! But we have to deliver for us, Stewart-Ford"

"But I was surrounded that day by a loving and supportive wife, and two very little boys, Mark and Paul.

"I have been a very fortunate man. Motor racing has been my passion. The sport blessed me and my family with privileges, material benefits and opportunities which have allowed me to fulfil so many dreams. There might never

From the top: Jackie didn't take long to teach Paul a trick or two about racing. Paul put the lessons to good use, and Jackie was proud to drive with him in a demonstration run for the press. Wife Helen, little Mark and Paul listen to Jackie announcing his retirement in 1973. A tough challenge lies ahead

AUTOSPORT

have been a Stewart-Ford team if Ken Tyrrell had not asked me to drive a Formula 3 car at Goodwood in 1964.

"There might never have been a Stewart-Ford team had not Walter Hayes put me under contract to the Ford Motor Company in 1964. And, in particular, we could not have reached the starting point for what has been a huge adventure without Neil Ressler, the vice-president of Advanced Vehicle Technology for Ford Automotive Operations.

"To have participated in this adventure with my own flesh and blood has been particularly nice. To do it together with Paul has been terrific. I wouldn't have done it without him, and I don't think I *could* have done it without him.

"And also to have my younger son Mark, who has a video production company, making a video which is going to go out as a TV special – it's been a whole family project. Poor Helen has been left a lot on her own, but she's been well used to that as a racing driver's wife, and she is long on patience.

"I just think it's been a great thrill for all of us – and the beginning of what I am sure will be a great challenge...." ◼

PAUL ON

Jackie

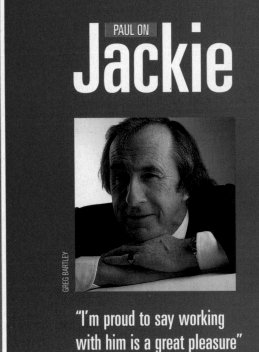

GREG BARTLEY

"I'm proud to say working with him is a great pleasure"

I think it is pretty obvious from the very fact that my father and I have worked together on these two projects, Paul Stewart Racing and the new team, that we are a close-knit family – even though I don't believe it is any secret he didn't want me to go racing myself when I first expressed an interest.

He didn't like it. His reaction, clearly, was that he thought he'd got away with it and that I was too old to go into motor racing. He was opposed to it, I think, because he had survived unscathed through what was a most dangerous period in racing, and now here I was all set to repeat the process.

But I did go racing and enjoyed it enormously. I was privileged to race at Monaco in Formula 3 and to outqualify Michael Schumacher at Macau. Fantastic moments which gave me a great deal of satisfaction.

But all these things happened because, to put it bluntly, of my father's success in motorsport. Clearly I had to represent him in the right way. I had to put in the effort and commitment, because otherwise everyone would have said "Jackie's son is a waste of time" and I would have looked like a joke. That I could never have lived with.

But I don't feel that being Jackie's son is a burden at all. The only thing I do worry about is that I always want to feel I'm doing justice to his reputation. I would hate to feel I was tagging on and not contributing.

On many occasions I'm asked: "What's it like to work with your father?" Well, I'm proud to say that it really is an enormous pleasure. I think this is reflected by the way the team has come together and the way in which, I hope, it will continue to grow.

Ford leads way with "dream" partnership

Thirty years after its debut Formula One win, the 1967 Dutch Grand Prix, Ford is spearheading Formula One's drive into the 21st century with its unprecedented input into the development of the new Stewart-Ford SF-1 challenger.

Never before has a major manufacturer been so fully involved in all aspects of a grand prix car's creation – from complex computer design and integrated electronic management to its cockpit ergonomics and pit-car radio communications.

"Working in this way with a major manufacturer is something which everyone in Formula One dreams about," says Stewart GP's technical boss, Alan Jenkins. "It takes a lot of commitment, but Ford have shown themselves more than willing. They have enormous capabilities and we are still only just beginning to learn how to harness them."

Careful management of the airflow over the SF-1's chassis is just one critical area where Jenkins called heavily upon the expertise of Ford engineers at the company's American headquarters in Dearborn, Michigan. As a result, the car's high sidepods feature steeply raked inlets with an unusually-shaped leading edge to optimise engine cooling, while still meeting Formula One's rigorous side-impact regulations and making best use of the car's turning vanes. "Every aspect of the aerodynamic package has been carefully optimised by this painstaking process," Jenkins confirms, "and many innovative details have emerged as a result."

The technical characteristics of the SF-1 are simply mind-boggling. At speeds of up to 200mph, Ford's engine management system employs an on-board computer capable of 1.7 million commands *every second* – rather more powerful than the PC chained to your desk!

Ford's desire is to use the intense pressures of Formula One as a testing ground not only for the latest motoring technologies but also for its engineers. "Formula One encourages innovative approaches and quick, accurate responses," says director of European motorsport Martin Whitaker. "That can only improve every aspect of our products, our processes *and* our people."

FORD'S V10 – A WHOLE YEAR BETTER

Developed by long-term partners Cosworth, the Ford Zetec-R V10 which powers the Stewart-Ford SF-1 is a very different engine from the one that began the 1996 season. During the winter, Cosworth expanded its Formula One engineering team to speed its development, and the Zetec-R now boasts airflow improvements (from revised inlet and exhaust port design), higher combustion efficiency and reduced frictional losses. Working closely with Stewart on the engine's installation, Ford and Cosworth have also developed new components such as cam covers, oil inlet and outlet castings and a revised flywheel.

ZETEC-R V10 TECHNICAL SPECIFICATION
No of cylinders: 10; Configuration: 72-degree vee
No of valves: 40
Capacity: 2998cc
Length: 605mm
Width: 520mm
Height: 460mm
Weight: 120kg
Cylinder block & pistons: aluminium
Crankshaft: steel

GREG BARTLEY

Sponsor-friendly

By the time of the SF-1's official launch on 10 December 1996, Jackie and Paul Stewart were able to confirm that they had covered this season's Stewart-Ford racing budget with the sponsorship deals that emblazon the car.

By then, the budget had already been committed for 1997 from Ford Motor Company, the HSBC Group (one of the world's leading international banking and financial services organisations), Visit Malaysia – reflecting backing from the Malaysian government in the promotion of the country as a business and tourist destination – plus Texaco fuel and lubricants, Sanyo and Hertz.

Crucially, Jackie Stewart says any sponsor involved with the Stewart-Ford

FOUR FABULOUS FORD FACTS

■ Before the Zetec-R V10 had even run in a car for the first time (on 16 January, 1996), it had already done 329 hours and 49 minutes on Cosworth's test beds.
■ When revving at its current maximum of 16,500rpm, an explosion occurs in one of the engine's combustion chambers every 0.0007 seconds.
■ In 1996, the Zetec-R V10 was on full throttle for the longest time during the German GP at Hockenheim: 50 minutes out of a total race time of 80 minutes.
■ The engine is fully rebuilt after every 250 miles of running (approximately two hours of track time), and each rebuild takes Cosworth technicians a total of around 200 hours....

White? Not quite

The pressures of building a completely new grand prix car from scratch played havoc even with the job of the SF-1's livery designers. With a month to go before its launch and the car still in pieces, templates had to be taken from the 50% wind tunnel model. Sadly, the model was available for this job only between nine at night and four the next morning....

The car's base colour white was selected for its TV visibility and unique ability to show off sponsors' full corporate colours. But that's not all: the particular shade of 'soft white' (cut with a little ochre) was mixed to reduce glare on camera, while the red, green and blue of the tartan were also tweaked for maximum effect.

Incidentally, choosing white also means the weight of the SF-1's livery is among the lowest on the grid!

MARTYN ELFORD

Designer Alan Jenkins on the launch of the SF-1: "The last 24 hours were totally sleepless. When it touched ground for the first time, at 5am on launch day, fifty of us were there to see it. A great moment."

19 December, 1996: a moment of history. The Stewart-Ford SF-1 turns a wheel in anger for the first time in the pouring rain at Ford's Boreham test facility. The run also marked the first time any 1997 Formula One car had been seen in action. Rubens Barrichello was the lucky driver – Jan Magnussen had to wait until after Christmas....

JON NICHOLSON

DRIVER BRIEFING

NO 22: RUBENS BARRICHELLO

BORN 23 May, 1972; Brazil.
CAREER HIGHS
1984: Brazilian junior kart championship runner-up.
1985-'86: Fourth in overall Brazilian kart championship ('85), winner Category A ('86).
1987-88: Brazilian kart champion, '87 and '88. 1987 – 125cc South American champion; ninth in world championship.
1989: Brazilian Formula Ford championship, fourth overall.
1990: GM Lotus Euroseries with Draco Racing. Six wins out of 11 races, seven pole positions, seven fastest laps.
1991: British Formula 3 champion with West Surrey Racing. Four wins from 15 races, nine pole positions, seven fastest laps and four track records.
1992: Third in FIA International F3000 Championship with Il Barone Rampante.
1993-96: FIA Formula One World Championship (all four seasons with Jordan). 17th overall in '93, then sixth in '94; eighth overall for past two years.

Jackie banks on bigger business

team will get more than simply global television exposure for their investment.

"The biggest thing for us is to give our partners value for money by creating new business opportunities for them," he explains. "For example, we believe HSBC, operating in 76 countries around the world, will generate a lot more incremental business than the amount they spend on the Stewart-Ford team.

"To bring more people over to Malaysia is also a priority. And it's good to be starting with Bridgestone tyres. Sanyo, on the other hand, are old professionals at

ALLSPORT

Announcement of the HSBC deal

Formula One, as are Texaco – indeed, we regard it as something of a coup that we have got them aboard, as another huge global player with 22,000 outlets.

"That is," Jackie is quick to add, "22,000 opportunities for exposure for *all* our sponsors....

"Of course, Ford Motor Company is our major partner," he says. "Without them, we simply could not have done all this. The fact that I am still with Ford after a 32-year relationship says it all. They have been absolute giants in putting together our particular set of jigsaw puzzles."

JACKIE'S VIEW

"**Only 24 years old**, and already he has four years of Formula One experience under his belt – impressive by any standards. A man with great potential, as was seen when he won the 1991 British F3 title and was competitive in F3000. But I think people might have been expecting too much too soon. Racing drivers *are* tough; they take a lot of knocks driving Formula One cars with no suspension movement. But mentally they can be very fragile. Drivers need special handling, and I don't think Rubens has yet realised all his latent potential. I think he's quite vulnerable and that hasn't been recognised in the past."

YES, IT'S A GENUINE TARTAN. WITH A PROUD HISTORY, TOO....

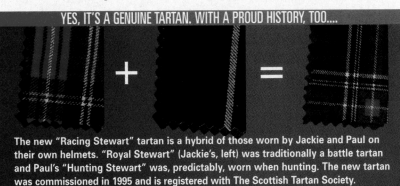

The new "Racing Stewart" tartan is a hybrid of those worn by Jackie and Paul on their own helmets. "Royal Stewart" (Jackie's, left) was traditionally a battle tartan and Paul's "Hunting Stewart" was, predictably, worn when hunting. The new tartan was commissioned in 1995 and is registered with The Scottish Tartan Society.

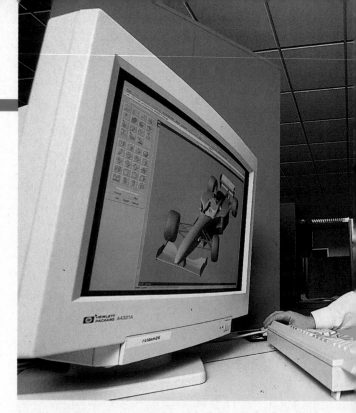

DRIVER BRIEFING

NO 23: JAN MAGNUSSEN

BORN 4 July, 1973; Denmark.
CAREER HIGHS
1984-'86: Danish karting champion.
1987: Junior world karting champion.
1988: Winner of Austrian Kart GP.
1989: Junior world karting champion.
1990: Senior world karting champion.
1991: Formula Ford debut.
1992: Third in British Formula Ford championship, seven wins. Winner Formula Ford Festival at Brands.
1993: Opel Lotus European series. F3 debut with Paul Stewart Racing: fourth and third in two races entered.
1994: British F3 champion with Paul Stewart Racing, winning 14 out of 18! First Formula One test: McLaren.
1995: McLaren Formula One team test driver. Formula One debut in Pacific GP, 10th. International Touring Car series runner-up, despite earlier broken leg!
1996: McLaren test driver. Four Indycar races in works Penske.

JACKIE'S VIEW

"Jan is only 23, yet already a three-time world champion kartist. He also became British F3 champion in dominant style. He has as much talent in a racing car as I've ever seen – with as good a head as anybody I've ever seen in this sport. I don't think he ever wanted to go touring car racing; he shouldn't have left single-seaters. But he thought he would get a lot of Formula One seat time, which did not happen. I think that, in turn, affected his attitude towards touring cars, because he saw it as a 'second best' situation. I believe that we have the ability to motivate Jan, and create for him what I sincerely believe will be a springboard to major success."

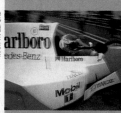

Right: Stewart's information-technology expert, systems manager Steve Nevey, checks on the new car via the Unigraphics CAD system. The only time an image is generated on paper is to aid a supplier without such technology....

DARREN HEATH

Put down that pencil, you CAD!

"To the best of my knowledge, this is the first Formula One car to have been entirely designed by computer from the outset." Jackie Stewart's assertion is a stark reminder of the philosophy that drives the Stewart-Ford alliance. But this desire to employ the very latest technology would have been impossible without the computer hardware and software made available by the team's technical partners.

"Having committed ourselves 100% to computer-aided design (CAD)," says Stewart's IT systems manager Steve Nevey, "we immediately forged a strong partnership with EDS, who provided our Unigraphics CAD software system. As strategic partners, they have *stayed* involved, constantly monitoring and updating the system to suit our precise requirements. That's the real advantage of this kind of sponsorship arrangement.

"We have a similar relationship with Hewlett-Packard. Not only do they provide all of our computer hardware (a very considerable investment in this high-tech team), but the heads of their California laboratories have already been over to discuss development projects. They're particularly strong on measurement, so they asked us what we'd like to measure that is currently out of reach. Hopefully we'll be able to acquire some fairly unusual data before long."

MSC complete Stewart-Ford's triumvirate of computer partners – its Patran system allows the team to simulate stress tests on newly-designed components, saving all-important time in the intensive (and never-ending) development process required by Formula One.

"The reason these companies enjoy working with us," Nevey adds, "is that we represent a fascinating model of a high-tech manufacturing industry. And since our priority is to reduce lead times in all areas of design and production, we're constantly looking to hone all our systems – which can only benefit them as well."

Is it a bird...?

No, it's the Stewart-Ford logo, conceived and generated by ace London design consultants Carter Wong & Partners – who also created the logo for Formula One's governing body, the FIA. The company's designs also adorn many well-known high-street products. The Stewart-Ford logo was completed over the latter half of 1996.

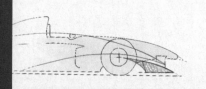

The origins of the Stewart-Ford logo can be found in profile drawings of the SF-1 itself. Early sketches show how the 'nose' of the logo approximates the front end of the new car.

MARTYN ELFORD

"So, what do *you* want to do when you grow up?" Two youthful observers at the SF-1 launch were Paul Stewart's toddler Dylan (he ended up posing in the cockpit for photos!) and HRH Princess Anne's son Peter Phillips, who's been working with the team.

FACTORY VISIT

'Interviews and shopping lists....' How to set up a new F1 team

The speed and directness of Ford's decision to partner this all-new team contradicts any tendency to portray the huge multinational company as a lumbering, conservative giant. The deal was not finalised until January 1996, yet the first Stewart-Ford car was running on the track before the end of that year.

Such a momentous achievement relies heavily on assembling the right team as quickly as possible. Indeed, as Stewart's technical chief Alan Jenkins points out: "In many respects, this project has been more about assembling a design and technical team than building a car.

"We started literally with an empty room. At one stage, Paul (Stewart) and I were doing nothing but interviewing. We have a staff of over 100 now, but to reach this level we've had to interview well over double that number."

Of the current staff (soon to go up significantly again as the test team is established), around half have come from elsewhere on the Formula One grid, bringing with them crucial experience for the fledgling organisation. Their reward has been an opportunity to shape the team's development.

"Perhaps where they've been before," suggests team manager

Dave Stubbs, "they might not have had the opportunity to put their opinions forward. Whereas we're on a fairly steep learning curve, and we're pretty open minded. It's been a golden opportunity to hand-pick people and put the right team together, and in that sense I think we've been pretty fortunate. It's worked."

Stewart's Milton Keynes base has more than doubled in size to accommodate the Formula One team, despite the termination of the Formula 3000 arm of Paul Stewart Racing. Little of the F3000 equipment was transferable, which meant one huge shopping list had to be drawn up...

"We went along to the Nürburgring race last year," Stubbs recalls, "to see what other people used. Then the chief truckie and I went to Canada to see how things operate these days at a flyaway race. The list of equipment we drew up was massive – everything from transporters to tool kits!

"Obviously, when you go and look in someone else's garage, they don't let you poke around too much. But I don't think we've left anything out. As we've brought in people from other teams, they have helped us complete any bits of the jigsaw that might have been missing...."

The first of the team's two artics arrived last December

Designing Swiftly on both sides of the Pond...

The Swift wind tunnel, used by Stewart-Ford to test its 50% prototype model of the SF-1, is acknowledged as the best of its kind in the world today. And its location across the Atlantic in San Clemente, California, highlighted another crucial benefit of the team's computerised design philosophy.

"A critical aspect of our CAD system," says Steve Nevey, "is that everyone works off one database. That includes the guys in California. They were connected to the factory by modem, so if an update was made in the factory, our aerodynamicist over there, Egbhal Hamidy (previously Adrian Newey's number two at Williams), could see it in pretty much real time."

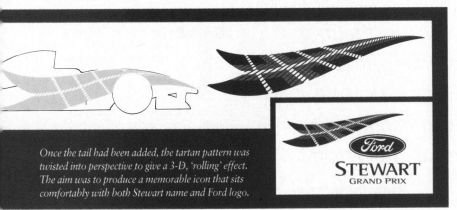

Once the tail had been added, the tartan pattern was twisted into perspective to give a 3-D, 'rolling' effect. The aim was to produce a memorable icon that sits comfortably with both Stewart name and Ford logo.

STEWART GRAND PRIX

A TEAM OF RACERS

The size of the Stewart-Ford team is, says Dave Stubbs, very much on a par with the rest of the Formula One grid. "We've just got fewer people on the manufacturing side, because we aren't doing so much in-house yet...."

The race team's structure breaks down like this: Overall organisation by team manager Stubbs and technical team manager Andy Miller. Technical director: Alan Jenkins. One senior engineer; two race engineers; two data loggers. One chief mechanic; six mechanics (three for each race car); two gearbox engineers; three mechanics for the spare car. Six truckies for three trucks (two artics for the cars and one rigid to carry pit gear).

Testing, testing....

Outside a race, the most telling time for a Formula One car is during testing. COLIN GOODWIN *follows every step of the SF-1's first test at Silverstone*

PHOTOS: DARREN HEATH

Today is the first time that Stewart-Ford's new car will run in anger. Almost one month ago it briefly turned its wheels, in the pouring rain, at Ford's Boreham proving ground in Essex. Then, the team wanted to check the car's systems with a few up-and-down runs. Rubens Barrichello did the driving, and the exercise went well.

There is, after all, an enormous amount of technical equipment that can, and does, go wrong, even with

well-proven Formula One cars, never mind a brand new one. So there is always a degree of trepidation before a car's first run. However, the team had very good reason to be pleased with that first outing at Boreham.

Today, we're here for a much more extensive test, and the evidence of that is obvious. The marquee that the team has erected next to Silverstone's South Circuit is crammed full of people. I've never seen a pit so crowded. People from Ford, from Cosworth, from Bridgestone, computer wizards, telemetry specialists

and more. This is what Formula One is about these days; not just a few key people, but a mass of experts and suppliers each making a contribution to the common cause.

A Formula One car at rest in its pit looks strangely as though it is in intensive care. From all over it come cables, tubes and hoses. A scaffold-like gantry over the car guides a thick umbilical cord from the car's black boxes to a bank of seven computers – two for data storage, two for gearbox and drive-by-wire, two for engine analysis and

one for engine calibration. A small cable goes to a lap-top computer that is used – along with a hand throttle – to start the engine.

At the back of the car a mechanic is warming the gearbox with a serious-looking hot air blower. This is not only to warm up the oil, but also to pre-heat the casing and bearings. The gearbox is built to such close tolerances that running from stone cold would do it no good at all. Eventually, all the systems have been checked, the gearbox sufficiently pre-heated and it's time to start the engine.

A portable starter motor with a long shaft is inserted into a slot at the back of the transmission. No one needs to be in the car, as the Cosworth technician can start it with his hand throttle and lap-top computer.

The Zetec-R V10 bangs and pops but doesn't start. It's pretty cold here, and it seems that the engine needs more fuel pressure and the gearbox is still a bit on the chilly side. An industrial heater is aimed at the rear of the car and an electric pump is plugged into the car's fuel filler to boost fuel pressure. Within minutes the V10 cranks into wailing life. Once it has run for a few minutes and has been checked for leaks, it is time to install the driver.

For non-Formula One people the drivers are the key figures, the heroes, the talents, the men whose relative merits are discussed over pints. In this world, the nitty gritty of Formula One, they are just another component. One that's difficult to control and one that can cause the biggest havoc. A single mistake from the driver can means hundreds of hours' extra work for the team.

Rubens Barrichello will be taking it easy here, though. It is the first test; really a systems shake-down before the team departs in a few days for Jerez in Spain for a full test session. Besides, he will be unpopular if he breaks the 75mph speed limit. I'm not joking. This is one of the many bizarre aspects of modern grand prix racing. The FIA, Formula One's governing body, says: No testing on non-FIA-approved circuits. Now, since the Silverstone Grand Prix Circuit currently has the road menders in, Stewart-Ford has to use the South Circuit, only about three-quarters of which is common with the Grand Prix circuit. For the section that isn't, there's a 120km/h speed limit, enforced by a radar gun....

Chassis No1 crackles and wails out of the marquee into the bright sunshine, the experienced Brazilian slipping the hand clutch and keeping the Zetec-R V10 lit by the fly-by-wire throttle. We had a late start this morning because this area showed some teething troubles at the factory last night, which meant an all-nighter for the team. Such is the Formula One life, especially in a brand-new équipe with a brand-new car.

Barrichello does one lap and then comes in. This is standard procedure for the first run of the day, to check whether all is well with the car. It is, so after swapping the slicks for wets he goes out for another three laps. The tyres are a source of much interest. The new Bridgestones could help

Above: Jackie Stewart started and ended the day a happy man.
Above left: Seldom has a car attracted so many people to the pits.
Middle left: Jan Magnussen discusses the SF-1 with a team technician.
Bottom left: the moment that Jan Magnussen has been looking forward to: in the SF-1's cockpit with Silverstone awaiting him

to give Stewart-Ford a very useful boost.

Still no problems. This is impressive. It's a shame about the speed limit, though. It robs those in the pits of the joy of hearing up close their creation emitting all its anger. More importantly, it means no meaningful times can be taken and limits how hard the car can be pushed. There is

"The car sounds fantastic. You can hear it around the back of the circuit, the gears slotting in neatly. The team looks relaxed"

time for another five laps, on slicks again, before the lunch break.

Nine laps, no problems. If this doesn't sound that much of an achievement, it certainly is. These cars are massively complicated. This has more to do with the high-tech on-board computers than with the way that grand prix cars are put together. All it needs is for the car's black box to fail to communicate properly with the engine's black box and the gears

won't engage. I've seen Williams' engineers spend ages trying to sort out just this problem. On a tried and tested car, to boot.

After lunch it is Jan Magnussen's turn in the cockpit. Magnussen hasn't driven a Formula One car since last summer but he does not look in the least bit fazed. The only time he has looked a little non-plussed today is when Jackie Stewart was giving him a talk about looking smart – his team-supplied Boss jacket was a poor fit, apparently. Stewart himself is wearing a hat entirely appropriate for the freezing conditions, but it still looks rather curious. Yet the man that he is, Stewart is laughing off the wry comments about his excessively furry hat. He spends a lot of time laughing and joking, both of which are much needed in Formula One.

Magnussen goes out on wets for four laps. No stalling, just confidently out on to the track and then accelerating in a scream as soon as he's out of the speed limit area. The car sounds fantastic. You can hear it round the back of the circuit, the gears slotting in neatly. The team looks remarkably relaxed. Even with the thorough preparation Stewart-Ford puts

The insider's story

Today is really going to be a shakedown test. All we really need to know is that the thing starts, stops, changes gear and can go around a corner. It's a nuisance about this daft speed limit. We could do with running the car hard, bouncing it off a few kerbs, to see how well it holds together. Second thoughts, since we're going to Jerez in a couple of days and this is the only car we have, it's probably not such a bad thing.

"It's a mammoth task starting up a team from scratch. And it's not just a matter of building the cars. All the support equipment has to be acquired or built. We went to around four grands prix last year and had a nose in a few garages to see what people had. I've been out of Formula One since 1989 and this team is a total newcomer. We've had to get hold of these banks of computers, build the fuelling machine,

fabricate stands, trolleys, starters and much else.

"When the season starts at Melbourne in March we'll have three cars, and by Monaco there'll be four. That's the point at which we can think about setting up a test team. Without a test team you have a serious disadvantage.. The grands prix that are in far-flung places – such as Argentina – eat up valuable testing time. You really need to be testing back here at the same time. Still, we don't have our race team sorted yet, so it's a bit early to be worrying about a separate team altogether.

"Today has gone very well. Plenty can go wrong on a new car, but this one's been exceptionally well behaved. We haven't learnt as much as we could have had we been able to run at a pace, but at least we'll be going to Spain with a racing car that's fit. It's a good starting point."

David Stubbs, team manager

in, there is always the potential for terminal problems. So far, so very good.

Next time the young Dane goes out he's back in only one lap. The dash lights have gone out, the ones that give him the vital information about the car's health and function. A connection has most likely been disturbed when the steering wheel was taken off. It is soon fixed and he is out again. Five laps later he is back in, this time requesting a change in brake balance. The rears are locking up early, apparently. Normally, he would have a brake bias adjuster in the cockpit, but that hasn't been fitted yet so the mechanics carry out the job by adjusting the length of rods from the pedal to the master cylinder.

It's 3.30 now and there's a beautiful sunset unfolding across the Northamptonshire sky. It is getting colder, though, and no sooner has Magnussen left the pit than he's back. There's ice on the track. That's it for today.

And what a successful day it has been for Stewart-Ford. One small skirmish in a long campaign, but a promising note on which to start the long haul to success on the race track. ◾

Pride
AND
joy

Technical boss Alan Jenkins had to design a new Formula One car from scratch – and create the factory that could produce more like it. He explains how

BY STEVE CROPLEY. PHOTOS: DARREN HEATH

When, last December, Paul and Jackie Stewart drew back the tartan cover to reveal the first ever Stewart-Ford grand prix car, one of the widest smiles among the onlookers was worn by Alan Jenkins, the new team's technical director. The event was public confirmation that he had not only brought a new Formula One car to life, he'd also successfully designed the factory that could produce more like it.

When 41-year-old Jenkins joined Stewart at the beginning of March 1996, the size of his task was far larger than the one most Formula One designers face. As well as devising a car that would meet both the team's expectations and budget, he was charged with recruiting the best possible design team, then staffing and devising an affordable manufacturing system.

Fortunately, Jenkins already had plenty of experience in each area. An industrial designer by training, he joined Ron Dennis and John Barnard at McLaren in the early 1980s, and was a key member of that team through its period of greatest expansion and success. In the middle 1980s he moved to Indycar

legends Penske, working at their design base in Dorset on the south coast of England. There, Jenkins drew the car that won Indianapolis (with Danny Sullivan driving) in 1985. After that, he set up the Onyx Formula One team, before joining Arrows in the late 1980s.

It was at Arrows that Jenkins first met Paul Stewart, when Stewart was invited to test a Formula One car towards the end of 1993. The pair got on well together. Jenkins, a wry sort of bloke not given to hyperbole, appreciated Stewart's

when the Stewart technical director's job came up towards the end of the year, he had no trouble deciding to take it.

"There were very few instructions about the kind of car I was to design," Jenkins says. "The limitations – in so far as there were any – were placed by the need to have a credible car on the grid at the start of 1997, and by the budget, which wasn't exactly a shoestring but wasn't excessive either. There were certainly ceilings on personnel. The idea was that I should avoid spending money

"There were very few instructions about the kind of car I was to design, beyond the need to have it on the grid at the start of 1997"

realistic attitude to his driving ability and racing aspirations. "Paul was much more straightforward than most of them," he says. "I liked him straight away."

During 1995 Jenkins learned of the Stewarts' Formula One aspirations – although he stayed committed to Arrows while it made its initial preparations. But

on a fully-equipped factory, but find suppliers who could deliver what we wanted at the right kind of quality."

By the end of his first month, Jenkins had begun recruiting his design staff. "We put priority on the race and design people, intending to build on that foundation as time went on. From the

The fast route to the grid

The Stewart-Ford SF-1 took comparatively little time to reach the track, given that its chief designer started work only nine months before the official launch, and the team's Formula One works had to be set up. Here are the key dates....

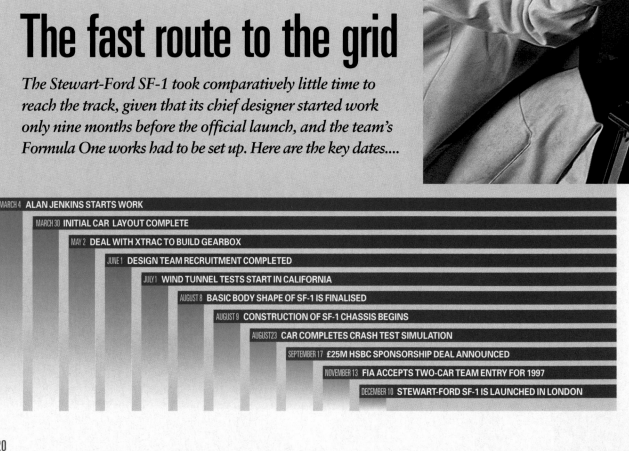

MARCH 4   ALAN JENKINS STARTS WORK

MARCH 30   INITIAL CAR LAYOUT COMPLETE

MAY 2   DEAL WITH XTRAC TO BUILD GEARBOX

JUNE 1   DESIGN TEAM RECRUITMENT COMPLETED

JULY 1   WIND TUNNEL TESTS START IN CALIFORNIA

AUGUST 8   BASIC BODY SHAPE OF SF-1 IS FINALISED

AUGUST 9   CONSTRUCTION OF SF-1 CHASSIS BEGINS

AUGUST 23   CAR COMPLETES CRASH TEST SIMULATION

SEPTEMBER 17   £25M HSBC SPONSORSHIP DEAL ANNOUNCED

NOVEMBER 13   FIA ACCEPTS TWO-CAR TEAM ENTRY FOR 1997

DECEMBER 10   STEWART-FORD SF-1 IS LAUNCHED IN LONDON

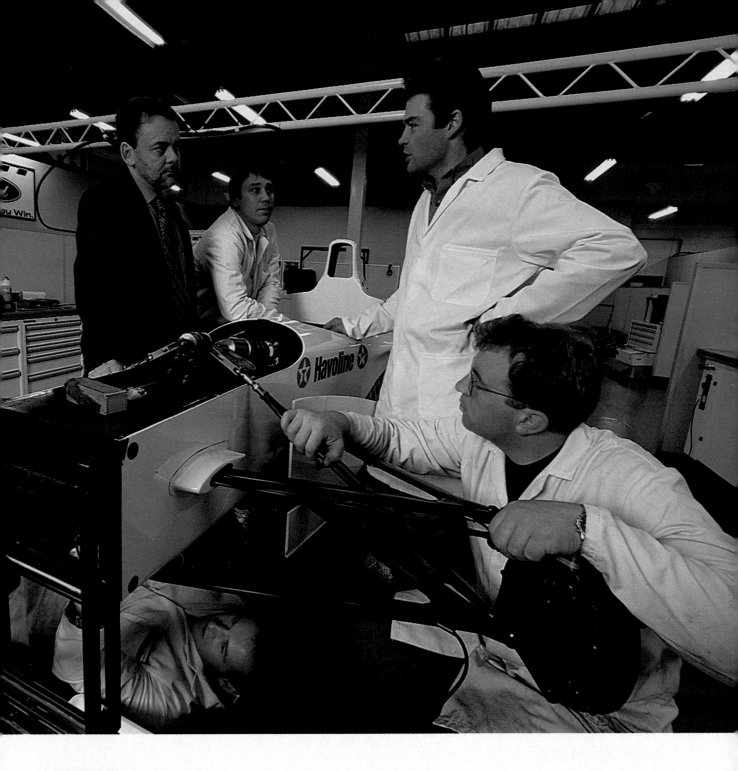

Main picture: team manager Dave Stubbs oversees the stripping down of the first SF-1 after its debut runs at Ford's Boreham facility on 19 December 1996

beginning, we decided to take only the best: if we couldn't get fifteen good people, we'd make do with twelve until the right ones came along." Inevitably, some Stewart-Ford people have come from other teams; there are staff from Benetton, Ferrari, Williams and Arrows, among others.

The layout of Jenkins' first Stewart-Ford car, the SF-1, mirrors current grand prix practice. It consists of a carbon fibre monocoque "tub" for the driver, which carries the Ford Zetec-R V10 engine and six-speed longitudinal gearbox

(unique to Stewart-Ford) as fully stressed members. Front and rear suspensions are by double wishbones with spring/damper units mounted inboard. Weights and major dimensions are tightly dictated by the legislation of Formula One's governing body, the FIA but, like previous Jenkins cars, the SF-1 features elegant design details that reflect their creator's early grounding in product design.

Despite the call for a car whose major components were sourced largely from suppliers, Jenkins changed the rules in two major ways. Firstly, he argued

> "I think our car is up with the best on aerodynamics. I don't believe we're going to give anything away"

through a plan to build a half-size wind tunnel model (only the richest teams make them so big) and test it at the Swift Engineering wind tunnel in California, the most advanced in the business. Secondly, he got the Stewarts to agree to build the chassis in-house.

The use of a 50% model reflects Jenkins' career-long preoccupation with the science of aerodynamics. He still believes it possible to steal a march on the best of the opposition in this area.

Naturally, the technical director won't reveal exactly where his design tweaks are (at launch, several areas of the SF-1's rear bodywork remained shrouded in tartan fabric) but the team's priorities are evident from the hiring of Egbhal Hamidy, an aerodynamics specialist who

was formerly number two to Adrian Newey at Williams. "I think our car is up with the best on aerodynamics," says Jenkins. "I don't believe we're going to give anything away."

While proceeding with initial design work – "getting the large lumps in the right place" – Jenkins' early task was to work out a realistic timetable for the car's production. "We found out early on that the wind tunnel would become available from 1 July, and we based everything around that. The things which take longest are the chassis and the gearbox, so we worked out schedules for those first, and came up with a car launch date of 18 December. Somebody said that was a week too late, so we adjusted things and made it the 10th."

The SF-1 was duly launched on that date – having been completed for the first time at just 5am the same morning....

Left: the shapely SF-1 sits proudly on its London launch pad. Right: the tartan trim cockpit uses the latest in computerised ergonomics to ensure a comfortable fit for its drivers.
Below: the exhaust area of a grand prix car is critical in achieving maximum levels of downforce.
Below left: the SF-1's detachable cockpit display

As well as refocusing the Stewarts' approach to aerodynamics, Jenkins also persuaded them to build the carbon fibre chassis in a well-equipped workshop he ran across by chance, just a mile from the team's headquarters in Milton Keynes, 25 miles north of London. "Building the chassis ourselves was an enormous advantage," he says. "It meant we could react to small, subtle issues that continually arose as the design proceeded."

Jenkins, like the Stewarts, is cautious about predicting success for his new car. After more than 15 years in the racing car business, he knows it doesn't come easily. But that same experienced eye also helps him recognise a team which is working well together, and he's confident about the prospects of Stewart-Ford in the longer term.

"There's a lot of people here who know what it takes to win," he says. "Let's just say I think we're going to cause quite a few surprises."

Forward with Ford

Stewart's technical commitment has, says Alan Jenkins, been matched all the way by its partners at Ford

A debutant it may be in technical terms, but the Stewart-Ford team draws on the resources of some of the biggest guns around. Principal among them is of course Ford, global car maker and a long-time backer of both Stewarts in racing.

"We've got an enormous commitment from Ford's top management," says SF-1 designer Jenkins. "They are really enthusiastic about the project. Neil Ressler, their technical chief, has been particularly supportive. Initially, some people were a bit hesitant about working around their differences, but Ressler told them they just had to get in there and make the thing work. So they did.

"Now we've got genuine co-operation going on wherever you look. Our car's fly-by-wire throttle is a terrific example. The software was written by Ford in Dearborn, Michigan. The electronics are in a box made by PI Research in Cambridge. The whole thing was tested on one of Cosworth's dynamometers, and now we're packaging it into the car here in Milton Keynes. That's co-operation for you!"

Stewart-Ford has also made other, unexpectedly early steps forward with the car's electronics. Right from the first grand prix, it is using what Jenkins describes as "complete unique trackside computer workstations", built from scratch exclusively for the team. Meanwhile, Stewart-Ford and engine builders Cosworth have rationalised their data collection systems so that both sets of engineers can work in harmony.

"In the end," concludes Jenkins simply, "everybody in the team just wants to win."

Since powering Michael Schumacher to the World Drivers' Championship in 1994, Ford has had only moderate success in Formula One over the past two seasons. But now its bedrock involvement in the Stewart-Ford team indicates a serious and vigorous effort by the global car maker to re-assert its position as a leading force in motor racing's most demanding discipline.

The decision to endorse its confidence in Jackie and Paul Stewart's ability with a five-year contract signals that Ford is more serious than ever about its Formula One investment.

"You have to remember that the 1997 Formula One season represents a tremendous milestone for the Ford Motor Company," explains Martin Whitaker, the company's director of European motorsport.

"It marks the 30th anniversary of Ford's first victory in grand prix racing. As a company, we've accomplished a great deal in the intervening three decades, with a record 174 Formula One victories and 13 World Drivers' Championships to our credit.

"That said, you bask at your peril in the glow of past glories in a sport as competitive as Formula One motor racing. With that thought in mind, Ford has entered into a long-term partnership with the brand-new Formula One team formed by Jackie and Paul Stewart.

"Announced at the beginning of 1996, this new venture represents a commitment to the sport above and beyond anything Ford has undertaken previously. For the first time, the company is a true partner with its chosen 'works' team in grand prix racing.

"Far from simply supplying its Zetec-R V10 engine on an exclusive basis, Ford has been able to bring many of its advanced engineering skills to bear on the project. As a result, the Stewart-Ford SF-1 benefits from significant Ford input in such key areas as suspension and chassis design, aerodynamics and electronics," observes Whitaker.

The European motorsport boss believes Ford's involvement with Stewart has stimulated its entire approach to Formula One. It is, he says, no longer simply about participation but, in the long term, about displaying the levels of technical capability required to win a world championship.

"The most important aspect of the Stewart-Ford partnership is to show that Ford have become firmly recommitted to Formula One. I think that, since Michael Schumacher won the 1994 World Championship in a Benetton-Ford (a triumph described by many people in the sport as Formula One's best-kept secret), Ford in many ways have lost the impetus behind their involvement in Formula One. We've had two years in the wilderness, if you like, and now we're emerging with renewed determination."

Whitaker concedes that, at times during 1996 – the debut season for the

Ford's Formula One roll of honour

DRIVERS

The following have won the World Drivers' Championship with Ford power:

Graham Hill: 1968
Jackie Stewart: 1969, 1971, 1973
Jochen Rindt: 1970
Emerson Fittipaldi: 1972, 1974
James Hunt: 1976
Mario Andretti: 1978
Alan Jones: 1980
Nelson Piquet: 1981
Keke Rosberg: 1982
Michael Schumacher: 1994.

Other drivers to have contributed to Ford's record total of 174 Grand Prix victories include: Ronnie Peterson, 10 (Lotus-Ford, March-Ford); Denny Hulme, 8 (McLaren-Ford); Jody Scheckter, 7 (McLaren-Ford, Wolf-Ford); Jim Clark, 5 (Lotus-Ford); Ayrton Senna, 5 (McLaren-Ford); John Watson, 5 (Penske-Ford, McLaren-Ford); Jacques Laffite, 3 (Ligier-Ford).

CONSTRUCTORS

The following have won World Constructors' Championships with Ford power:

Lotus: 1968, 1970, 1972, 1973, 1978
Matra: 1969
Tyrrell: 1971
McLaren: 1974
Williams: 1980, 1981.

Thirty years after its landmark first Formula One victory, Ford goes into the 1997 season more motivated than ever. ALAN HENRY finds out why

Chip OFF THE OLD block

1997. We've still got further to go but the development process is well on course. We have an engine which is far more driveable, and now we're looking for more horsepower."

Whitaker firmly believes that this sort of technological struggle is precisely what makes Formula One such a worthwhile exercise as far as the Ford Motor Company is concerned.

"Indeed, I think one of the clearest examples of Formula One's practical benefits to Ford is that it stands out as a perfect proving ground for the next generation of engineers," he explains.

"The timescale pressure in Formula One gives them the opportunity to turn things around in, say, six days which, under normal circumstances – inside mainstream engineering – they might not be asked to complete in six weeks, or even six months!"

And yet it remains the Ford Motor Company's personal, long-standing relationship with Jackie Stewart which provides the bond that holds this latest, high-profile Formula One deal together – reflecting a personal association between Jackie and Ford which extends back 32 years and pre-dates his own grand prix debut.

"Jackie and Paul now are very much part of the family," says Whitaker. "The long tradition of the Stewart family's relationship with Ford is central to this whole partnership, and there are tremendous benefits to be gained by everybody involved." ◾

Zetec-R V10 which powers the new Stewart-Ford SF-1 – Ford made less progress with the engine than had been anticipated. However, he reaffirms that engine builder Cosworth latterly has made some giant strides forward, particularly through its enhanced development programme over the winter months. This progress should pay significant dividends as the year unfolds.

"I think the 1996 season was a pretty big disappointment for us all," he says. "Because of our history, I think a lot of people expected us to come out of the box with a competitive engine. And so it came as a bit of a shock when we didn't, even though lots of other manufacturers have struggled with V10s in the past.

"But Cosworth have worked pretty damn' hard over the past few months to make sure the engine is competitive in

How involved is Ford in motorsport?

Alone among manufacturers, Ford is active in what are generally regarded as the four most demanding forms of motorsport in the world: the FIA Formula One World Championship, the CART PPG Indycar World Series, the FIA World Rally Championship and the NASCAR Winston Cup. Ford-powered cars have also won each of these championships. Add in the Slick 50 Formula Ford World Series and involvement in a number of national touring car and rally championships, and the extent of Ford's commitment to motorsport worldwide is clear.

The real winners, however, are Ford customers. It is they who ultimately benefit from lessons Ford engineers and designers learn from participation in top-level motor racing and rallying and are then able to incorporate into Ford production vehicles.

Red hot partners

In the heart of every winning Ford engine beats the technical expertise of Cosworth. What's the secret of its success?

BY STEVE CROPLEY. LEAD PHOTO: DARREN HEATH

DARREN HEATH

Above: the newly-developed Zetec-R V10 glows red hot on the Cosworth Racing dyno. Right: Ford's 3-litre, 10-cylinder Formula One engine is externally similar to the 1996 version, but features updated inlet and exhaust port design, as well as new cam covers, oil inlet and outlet castings and a revised flywheel

GREG BARTLEY

According to Nick Hayes, leader of the 200-strong Cosworth team that has created and developed Ford's Zetec-R V10 race engine, one of the best qualifications for a grand prix job is the ability to keep a secret.

Soft-voiced and mild-mannered, 36-year-old Hayes would make a Swiss banker look indiscreet. He believes the heat of grand prix competition isn't only felt at the track, but is evident in every Formula One race shop and design office across Europe. And, he says, serious Formula One insiders don't boast about their achievements, which is why he won't give precise details about his race engine, or allow detailed photographs of its internals.

"You never know when an idea that you may consider normal hasn't occurred to somebody else," he says. "I don't want to risk providing my rivals with answers or ideas they don't already have."

Despite this, quite a few key facts about the Ford Zetec-R V10 engine – which powered Sauber's cars in 1996 and will be used in improved form by Stewart-Ford in 1997 – have found their way on to the record. The engine has 10 cylinders, in two banks of five inclined to one another at an angle of "seventy-ish" degrees. Each cylinder's four valves are actuated by twin overhead camshafts, working with compressed air "springs" instead of the steel variety which are usual in lesser engines. The V10's fuel injection and electronic ignition are both controlled by a Ford engine management system, while its main components are made from aluminium, steel, titanium, magnesium and carbon.

"There are some other, more exotic materials in the engine which we don't talk about because we like to think the opposition don't have them," says Hayes. "But in reality I think they probably do...."

Most race engine makers have the majority of their components produced by outside suppliers, but Cosworth

Racing, who also builds Ford engines for "customer" Formula One and Indycar use, has the facilities to produce and machine most of its own engine components. Blocks and heads are cast, using advanced (Cosworth-patented) techniques, at the company's foundry in Worcester. Engine design, development and build take place at Cosworth's Northampton headquarters, where Nick Hayes himself is based.

"We still buy some highly specialised components outside," he says. "Things like piston rings, ball bearings and conrod bolts. But we're more self sufficient than most of the others."

Planning for the Ford Zetec-R V10

"There are some exotic materials in the engine which we don't talk about because we like to think the opposition don't have them...."

began in the last week of January 1995, after Ford and Cosworth decided that the successor to Michael Schumacher's 1994 championship-winning V8 should have 10 cylinders. The engine was running by the first week of October that year, and powered Sauber cars through the 1996 season. The 1997 version – considerably developed internally though similar in appearance – is being used exclusively in Stewart-Ford's SF-1 cars.

Why did Cosworth decide on the change to V10? It was a difficult decision, says Hayes. "In a modern grand prix car, practically speaking, you've got a choice of V8, V10 or V12. All things being equal, the V12 is most powerful, but it is also

Cosworth

It's exactly 30 years since Ford's most enduring partner unleashed grand prix racing's most successful engine ever....

Cosworth Racing co-founders Keith Duckworth and Mike Costin first came together in spirit (and ultimately name) at the cramped premises of Colin Chapman's Lotus Engineering in north London. By the summer of 1958, the two men had resolved to go into business together.

Initially, Cosworth took on a range of projects, building the highly successful Formula Junior engine and elements of the Ford Cortina GT road car's power unit. Despite its founders' desire to keep the company small, their reputation grew,

The Ford-Cosworth DFV is readied for its debut outing at the 1967 Dutch GP. Formula One would never be the same again

AUTOSPORT

and so did the offers of race and road car projects.

Then, in the spring of 1965, Colin Chapman persuaded Ford to back the design of a new 3-litre Formula One engine. Chapman knew Duckworth was the man for the job, and so the Ford-Cosworth partnership was born. Duckworth was already working on a revolutionary new four-cylinder Formula 2 engine (the FVA), and its success paved the way for the engine that was to take Formula One by storm – the V8 Ford-Cosworth DFV.

Built initially for the Lotus 49, the engine had an immediate impact. On its Formula One debut, the 1967 Dutch Grand Prix, the Lotus driven by Graham Hill took pole – no other type of car would threaten the grid's number one spot for the rest of the year! Hill's team-mate Jim Clark won that first race, thus starting a record that would make the DFV (and its derivatives) grand prix racing's most successful engine ever. Its final victory – number 154 – came as late as 1983, when Keke Rosberg's Williams FW08C took the Monaco Grand Prix.

By 1989, Ford and Cosworth were back in the Formula One winners' circle, as Alessandro Nannini's Benetton B189 clinched the first win for the V8 HB engine. Then, in 1994, the 3.5-litre Zetec-R V8 powered Michael Schumacher to the world title, his Benetton B194 taking eight wins.

the biggest, weighs the most, needs the biggest radiators (which generate extra aerodynamic drag) and uses most fuel."

A V8 is the lightest and most compact, while it also uses less fuel than a V10 or V12. This, Hayes says, made it a very attractive option until mid-1993, when refuelling was reintroduced to Formula One. With low fuel consumption less of a priority, the V10 then became the preferred option, offering extra power potential without the ultimate size and weight disadvantages of a V12.

The exact power of a grand prix engine, and the rpm at which it operates, is information that's closely guarded by every Formula One team. But it's an open secret that today's "contender" engines produce well over 700bhp from their 3-litre capacity, and spin to more than 16,000rpm. But ask him to confirm such things, and all you'll get from Nick Hayes is an enigmatic smile. "Ultimate power isn't important," he says. "It's the performance of the total package that counts. If we could win races with 10 horsepower, we'd be happy to do that...."

When installed in a Formula One chassis, the Ford V10 must do more than simply produce power. As is normal grand prix design practice, it forms part of the car's actual structure, bolting rigidly to the back of the carbon fibre tub that carries the driver. At its other end, the clutch housing and gearbox are bolted on, with the rear suspension mounted directly to the gearbox. This is why, Hayes explains, both the engine block and its mounting systems have to be as stiff as possible. The overall rigidity of a car's chassis is a huge contributor to good handling.

Above: Nick Hayes, leader of the Zetec-R V10 design and development team, is one of six Cosworth engineers servicing the SF-1's power units at every grand prix this year.
Left: Cosworth's Northampton base is handily placed close to the Stewart factory

DARREN HEATH

design this tendency out, but it would make the whole engine heavier."

In 1997, Cosworth will maintain a pool of about 25 engines to back the three SF-1s (including the spare). "We take at least 10 engines to a race," says Hayes, "along with five Cosworth people besides myself. We'll have a race engineer for each car, a technician to run the data collection system, and two engine fitters.

"Practice laps before a grand prix are limited these days, but at some of the longer tracks each car still needs a new engine every day. So sometimes we'll have more than 10 engines on hand – especially if we've got some development units we want to run. But normally we'll race the spec' we think is likely to be most reliable."

"Practice laps are limited before a grand prix now, but at some of the longer tracks each car still needs a new engine every day"

Modern data collection systems mean Cosworth's people can monitor literally dozens of engine parameters as the car laps the track – rather more than the familiar temperature, pressure, rev and throttle settings that road-going motorists are used to.

"We keep an eye on things like the supply of compressed air for the engine's air valves," Hayes explains, "because if that looks like running out, we've got the option of calling the car in and replenishing the air supply – although, in a race, we probably wouldn't do that. Imagine how we'd feel if the car was doing well, then we called it in and found that only the sensor was at fault, not the system...."

If there's one central key to success in grands prix, Hayes believes, it's getting the car and engine to integrate as a package. Of course, that calls for close co-operation between a team and its engine builder – something very much on the combined agenda of Stewart-Ford and Cosworth Racing for the 1997 season.

"They are close to us geographically, and that helps," Hayes says. "But most of all, they are close to us in mind; they're our kind of people. They are completely determined to win races, and so are we." ■

Stiff it may be, but durable? In fact, a modern grand prix engine does not have to last very long. Not in road car terms, anyway. Cosworth limit their Zetec-R V10 engines strictly to 250 miles of running, and rebuild them comprehensively after that. "Quite a lot of an engine's high stress parts go straight into the bin, to be melted down and recycled, as soon as we've examined them for unusual wear or distortion," says Hayes.

"We expect big components like heads, blocks and crankshafts to be used more than once. Often we'll machine blocks and heads before they're used again, because the loads they've been subjected to make them move a little bit. We could

*From the moment Ford gave
the Stewarts the green light,
Paul Stewart has been juggling
all manner of balls (and phones).
Now, at last, he tells ALAN HENRY
what life's really been like....*

THE
Ring Master

LEAD PHOTOS: TERRY O'NEILL

Since retiring from race driving at the end of 1993, Paul Stewart's whole focus has been on taking the "family team" to fresh levels of competitive achievement. In particular, that meant graduating to the high-pressure world of grand prix racing.

Thus, the arrival of Stewart-Ford on the Formula One scene is itself the realisation of a dream. It also marks a personal milestone for Paul, who has worked tirelessly for more than a year, building the company infrastructure required to underpin the entire operation.

Once the new Stewart team began to develop, how did Paul and his father share out the myriad responsibilities involved in operating the new company?

"I don't think we ever said: 'Well, you do this, and I'll do that'," recalls Paul. "Things just seemed to evolve in a logical manner. But I suppose, because I was the one who was actually based here at our Milton Keynes factory, I was the one who – together with Rob Armstrong, our commercial director – had to co-ordinate how it was all going to be done.

"We created our proposal to Ford with the help of J Walter Thompson in Detroit.

"It was very hard in the last few days before the new car's launch. The guys were working through the night regularly, not leaving until 7am and then back by 11 the same morning!"

You must understand, this was the most important proposal we had ever made. There was an opportunity there, clearly – the climate seemed right.

"Before that we were just looking for opportunities. We'd been round the world exploring various things.... The interesting thing is, the exercise we went through each time helped shape the proposal that we ultimately put to Ford.

"It was a very elaborate proposal indeed – not something we could have dreamt up overnight, if you like. In retrospect, if we had gone in cold, I suspect it might not have worked.

"Once we'd got the initial go-ahead, as I said, the demarcation lines between my father and I were never clearly laid out. In some ways, I suppose you could

say that it would have been more difficult for me if my father had been based here at the factory. But because I was the one who *was* based here, that gave me the chance to take operational decisions which, had he been here, he might have taken himself."

Once the Stewart-Ford partnership was officially launched in January of last year, the delineation of responsibilities between father and son really became more established. Chairman Jackie and Rob Armstrong concentrated their efforts on the commercial side, while managing director Paul was kept busy organising the factory headquarters – including the recruitment of Alan Jenkins as the team's technical director.

"Working with Alan was very

important for me," says Paul. "So too, of course, was bringing in the other key personnel, interviewing, setting up the systems and so on. But the really exciting thing was how much interest the team's official launch attracted from so many highly qualified figures within the sport.

"There was also a fascinating degree of cross-fertilisation of ideas from all our new people. I think that could only have happened in a totally new Formula One environment such as this.

"Remember, we weren't working within an existing organisation that had established systems of operating. We really were setting up all of the structures to operate a new grand prix racing team as we went along!" ∎

Left: Checking the
gearbox after the
car's first test run.
Above: Painstaking
attention to detail
is a way of life

DARREN HEATH

Above: Technical team
manager Andy Miller (on
right) studies the finer points
of the SF-1 with engineering
manager Colin McGrory

DARREN HEATH

TERRY O'NEILL

Above: Jan Magnussen (on left) discovers that all
of the SF-1 carbon fibre monocoques are built
in-house. Right: Jan's team-mate Rubens Barrichello
inspects the 50% wind tunnel model

GREG BARTLEY

"Without Ford, Paul and I would
not have contemplated this move
into grand prix racing. Their support
is incalculable"

JACKIE STEWART, three times world champion,
at the launch of the Stewart-Ford SF-1

PHOTO: DARREN HEATH

RACING STEWART

RACING

MAURICE HAMILTON AND JON NICHOLSON

STEWART

THE BIRTH OF A GRAND PRIX TEAM

MACMILLAN

First published 1997 by Macmillan

an imprint of Macmillan Publishers Ltd
25 Eccleston Place, London SW1W 9NF
and Basingstoke

Associated companies throughout the world

ISBN 0 330 71609 4

1 3 5 7 9 8 6 4 2

A CIP catalogue record for this book is available from
the British Library.

Photographic reproduction by
Aylesbury Studios, Bromley, Kent
Printed and bound in Great Britain by
Butler & Tanner Ltd, Frome and London

CONTENTS

FOREWORD

For both of us, this book records an extremely important time in our lives. Through Maurice's eloquent pen and Jon's equally revealing camera, *Racing Stewart* captures the hard work, commitment and spirit invested in this project by our whole team. Only the most extraordinary collective effort – incredibly long working hours for extended periods – made it possible for the team to arrive in Melbourne on time and ready to practise, qualify both cars and race in the team's first-ever Grand Prix.

Everyone who joined the company was taking a chance – though they may not have realized it at the time! Many came from secure jobs to help create Stewart Grand Prix, adding their own vote of confidence to the judgement we ourselves were backing. Thankfully, that calculated risk proved well worth taking, especially in hindsight. The joy and relief felt by the whole team, both in the pit lane and back at base, when Rubens Barrichello crossed the line in second place at the Monaco Grand Prix for our first podium finish gave us all a magical high that, at least for both of us, will never be forgotten.

Qualifying fifth in Argentina and third in Canada were other superb achievements for a first-year team, but we all know the track ahead is not without its obstacles. Regular race finishes, for one thing, are the first essential step if we are to feature regularly in the points. As a brand-new team in Formula One, we knew it would not be easy – and we never promised more than we have already delivered.

As a company, Stewart Grand Prix has expanded rapidly, with growing pains kept to the minimum. Our approach to Formula One has also struck a chord with well-wishers around the world. Their numbers surprise us, and their support is greatly appreciated by us all.

We hope our readers will be impressed by what has been accomplished in such a short time, and we would both like to thank them and the many other people who have been a source of inspiration to us and to the entire team.

JACKIE AND PAUL STEWART
August, 1997

CHAPTER ONE

FLYING HIGH

IT WAS THE MOST UNLIKELY LOCATION for a significant piece of sporting history. A plain white tent on a barren airfield in Essex could scarcely be called Grand Prix racing at its most glamorous. Nothing glittered. Nobody had come to watch because outsiders were not welcome. This was not a show. A birth never is.

The pregnancy had, appropriately enough, taken nine months. Close members of the family were allowed inside the tent because only they could fully appreciate the sense of fulfilment which would come if everything went well. At eleven minutes past eleven on Thursday 19 December 1996 everyone held their breath. The first Grand Prix car from the house of Stewart was about to burst into life.

This was more than simply the rolling out of another Formula One machine. It was the start of a new era, the next phase in the creation of the Stewart motor racing dynasty by Jackie and his son Paul. It was the defining moment when Jackie Stewart moved from being one of the greatest drivers at the top of the sport to a Formula One team owner and constructor, about to start the climb all over again.

The first Grand Prix car from the house of Stewart was about to burst into life

No one was more acutely aware of the pitfalls. As he pulled back the flap of the tent and the car moved under its own power for the first time, Stewart knew what lay ahead. There would be moments of elation and periods of pleasure, but frustration and hardship would be the most consistent companions during this journey. Yet as the white Stewart-Ford accelerated gently onto the deserted runway and burbled into the misty drizzle the thrill was palpable.

Never mind that this was hardly a high-speed spectacle. Forget the bleak surroundings. After nine months of conception and nine months of growth, the Stewart-Ford was a runner. This was noisy proof that the new team meant business; that it was more than simply a famous name operating on a whim.

Jackie Stewart has described the creation of the team as the most difficult task he has ever undertaken. Considering the depth of his achievements at the wheel, that gives some idea of the endeavour involved. It also explains why the Scotsman had never contemplated the idea when reviewing his options at the time of his retirement from the cockpit in 1973.

He did not have a clear idea about what he wanted to do. All he knew was that motor racing, in any shape or form, was not a priority even though this branch of the sporting industry had been his life for more than a decade.

It had been lucrative, providing a comfortable living for him, his wife, Helen, and their sons, Paul and Mark. But it had also brought a great deal of pain and suffering, not so much on the physical side – Stewart never spilt a drop of blood during competition – but through the relentless trauma brought about by the sport's larcenous nature.

In 1970 alone he attended the funerals of Bruce McLaren, Piers Courage, and Jochen Rindt, close friends killed in racing cars. That grim sequence of events was merely one sad entry in a list of more than twenty accidents which had claimed the lives of his colleagues. More than anything before, it was the seemingly endless catalogue of despair in 1970 that had prompted Jackie to consider retiring from competition.

In April 1973, he made up his mind to finish at the end of the season. The last race, the United States Grand Prix, would be his hundredth World Championship Formula One race, a nice round number. In the end, the tally remained at ninety-nine. During practice for that race in upstate New York, Stewart's team-mate, François Cevert, was killed as the result of a particularly violent accident. The team withdrew immediately. Cevert was an utterly beguiling Frenchman with dark eyes and handsome features. He had sat at Jackie's right hand for three seasons; learned everything there was to know. By October 1973, he had matured enormously and could match everything the maestro had to offer. He was ready to take over the role as team leader. His terrible death was a tragic and untimely demonstration of the sport's omnipresent peril. Not that Jackie needed reminding.

As a leading driver, Stewart's role in the aftermath of a fatal crash was obvious. Helen's was less so, but Jackie had his wife's feelings very much in mind when deciding how best to occupy himself in retirement.

'It's difficult for people to understand today,' says Stewart. 'Fatal accidents, because of the enormous strides which have been made in safety on the cars and in trackside facilities, are thankfully few and far between. Twenty-five years ago, the regularity of it was absolutely horrendous. Far too often, Helen had to go to the hotel room of a friend on a Saturday or a Sunday afternoon and pack bags that would make just one more journey. Feeling she was intruding very deeply, she would nevertheless have to go through personal effects – sometimes very personal items – and put them in a suitcase and then begin to think about how to help a girlfriend who might not be there but who was suddenly without the person with whom she had hoped to share the rest of

Cevert's terrible death was a tragic and untimely demonstration of the sport's omnipresent peril

her life. Children would need looking after because the distraught mother could not cope; there would be funerals and memorial services to organize and attend.

'Helen was not so much playing a role; that's an oversimplification. She was witnessing the destruction of a family unit, but in a highly intense way. And while all of that was going on I was still racing. I didn't feel there was any way I could say, after I had retired, that I was going to continue in racing. I couldn't have said, "Don't worry. It's going to be all right now – but I'm going to run a racing team." Helen was ready to get away from going racing every weekend, the continuous global travel. She would have asked: "Why on earth do you want to run a racing team?" It would have been a very sensible question. In truth, the thought never entered my head.'

Twenty-three years later, Helen Stewart was thrown back into the turmoil of motor racing at its highest level as her husband and eldest son laid plans for a team which had almost crept up on them. Jackie's activities in the commercial world as consultant and spokesman for companies such as Goodyear, Elf, and Ford had kept him in touch with motor racing but that did not become a hands-on involvement until 1987, when Paul made a decision about his future.

Paul said he wanted to take up racing. Many parents, particularly fathers, might be pleased by the thought, but for Helen and Jackie it was the obvious nightmare for anyone intimately familiar with the risks. It seemed that this was pushing providence too far.

Life had been more than kind to the Stewart family. Jackie had raced at the highest level, had won three world championships and the respect which came with it. There had been bad times and there had been very sad times but in between came the undeniable thrill of taking a racing car to the limit, driving it faster than anyone else, and being handsomely rewarded. A garage owner's son from Dumbartonshire, Stewart had earned status and recognition the world over. He lived comfortably, but not extravagantly, in Switzerland, where the two boys were educated. Paul and Mark were charming and well mannered; a tribute to their upbringing in a loving family. And now Paul, at the age of twenty-one, wanted to venture into the dangerous arena from which his father had emerged unscathed. Jackie and Helen could have been forgiven for thinking their good luck might be about to run out.

There was only one answer. They had to give their blessing. Blocking Paul's efforts would simply divert him into the sport by another route, one which

Paul said he wanted to take up racing but for Helen and Jackie it was the obvious nightmare

might be neither suitable nor, more importantly, safe. It could also break up the close family unit which they prized so much. By giving reluctant approval, Jackie could at least monitor his son's progress and lend from a vast pool of knowledge which had been gathered the hard way. But that did not mean that Paul Stewart would be guaranteed an easy ride.

Motor racing dynasties are rarely successful. The exceptions are Graham and Damon Hill, Gilles and Jacques Villeneuve, and the Andretti and Unser families in the United States. The three sons of former World Champion Sir Jack Brabham have made little impact. Neither has Justin Bell, son of five-times Le Mans winner Derek Bell, nor Christian Fittipaldi, nephew of Emerson Fittipaldi. Natural talent is not handed down as a matter of course. But Jackie felt that his son should at least be allowed to discover the extent of his capabilities under reasonable circumstances. By helping to establish a foundation from which Paul could work, Jackie was being drawn back into his natural element. He may have kept a low profile, thus ensuring that Paul could establish his name in his own right, but it was obvious that Jackie was enjoying the return to familiar territory during this latest development in his fast-moving life.

Anxious not to smother his son's career at birth, he stayed away from Paul's first press launch. When a team was eventually formed in 1988 to provide a more stable and progressive base, it was known as Paul Stewart Racing. Paul's competitive aspirations took his rapidly expanding team through Formula Ford 2000, Formula Three, and into Formula 3000. Jackie could see the need to establish a flow of young drivers and engineers, a kind of motor racing academy which he referred to as their 'staircase of talent'. But at no stage did the thought of making the final step into Formula One enter the equation. Or, at least, not for Jackie.

Paul was more ambitious. Once he had stepped down from driving in 1993 in order to concentrate further on the team, he made a pact with himself to compete in a higher series by the end of the year. There were touring cars and Indycar racing to consider. But Formula One remained the ultimate goal. After taking counsel from John Barnard, the Technical Director at Ferrari, the Stewarts' plan reached an advanced stage in 1993 and the question of funding moved the project more firmly into Jackie's domain. He was convinced that the financial future lay with the Asia–Pacific region. By a process of elimination, Stewart concluded that he should target Malaysia. But how?

There were touring cars and Indycar racing to consider. But Formula One remained the ultimate goal

When Jackie narrowly missed selection for the British Olympic Clay Pigeon Shooting team in 1960 (two years before he took up motor racing) he little realized that his skill with a gun would stand him in good stead three decades later. By opening a shooting school at Gleneagles in Scotland and using it as a base for charity work with personalities and businesspeople, he automatically became a part of the social round at the highest level. It was while mulling over the Malaysian concept that he accepted an invitation from Lord King to join Sebastian de Ferranti and a number of heavy hitters from industry at a shoot on the Wartnaby estate. Respecting the opinion of former Chairman of British Airways, he sought his advice on the question of Malaysia. Lord King said the only answer was to go to the very top; Stewart should make an appointment with the Prime Minister, Dr Mahathir Mohamad.

Stewart was proposing to put together a Malaysian Grand Prix team, based in the United Kingdom but financed by Malaysia as a means of promoting the country and, among other things, its motor industry. Jackie and Paul, in consultation with Barnard, had created a business plan and a budget which would run to £24 million. Jackie was excited about the project and he was sure, given the chance, that he could pass on his enthusiasm to the Prime Minister.

'I had been granted twenty minutes; just the two of us,' he recalls. 'I stayed for an hour and fifteen minutes. Dr Mahathir was excited by it. When he asked me how soon we could do it, I replied that it would probably be 1997/98. He said that would not be soon enough. He was in a hurry to get things done.'

It was a typical response from the Prime Minister of a rapidly developing country, one which planned to host the Commonwealth Games in 1998 and had introduced a major programme of infrastructure investments, including a £2.5 billion international airport at the capital, Kuala Lumpur.

Stewart was asked to speak to Dr Mahathir's science adviser, followed later by a presentation in Kuala Lumpur to representatives from tourism, the motor manufacturer Proton, the country's public relations agency, and Petronas, the state-owned oil and petroleum company. Everyone expressed an interest.

Further cost analyses were prepared. A party from Malaysia flew to Britain to inspect the premises of Paul Stewart Racing in Milton Keynes. They also visited Cosworth the engine builders, Hewland the gearbox specialists, and Reynard the racing car constructors, with which the Stewarts had been doing business over the years. Then Paul Stewart Racing invited twenty-five guests (including the presidents of Proton and Petronas) to a race at Thruxton in

Stewart was proposing to put together a Malaysian Grand Prix team, based in the United Kingdom

Hampshire. As ever, the PSR cars, transporter, garage, and equipment were immaculately presented. And the team won the Formula Three race. They also won approval. A fax arrived, giving the provisional go-ahead for the Malaysian team.

Three weeks later, another fax arrived cancelling the project.

'It was a disappointment,' recalls Jackie, with perhaps a touch of under-statement. 'We had started to take on a design team and employ more people in other departments. Legal documents were in the process of being drawn up. I flew to Malaysia and went through the whole thing. But the problem was, the concept was completely new to them; nothing like a Grand Prix team existed in Malaysia and it was a difficult concept for them to grasp. £24 million per year was a lot of money for a government to commit to. Some people in racing might have responded by saying that they could do it cheaper. But you can't. From the very beginning we had made a commitment that if we could not do it properly, then we would not do it at all. Overall, it had been a very useful experience, but I thought that was it for us and Formula One for the time being.'

Nonetheless, Stewart had done an excellent job transmitting his enthusi-asm. The Malaysians were keen to know if they could host a Grand Prix. Stewart gave further presentations and finally brokered a meeting between Dr Mahathir and Bernie Ecclestone, the Formula One supremo, in London. A multi-year contract was agreed. Stewart did not have his Malaysian Formula One team but, thanks to the regular contact during a two and a half year period, a social bond had been created. Jackie would lunch with the Dr Mahathir when he visited Malaysia; they would meet in London and perhaps go to the theatre together. A link had been forged between Malaysia and Formula One. All was not lost.

Meanwhile, the Stewarts had thrown themselves into the pursuit of contin-uing excellence. Paul Stewart Racing had won several championships by now and Jackie was keen to see the team make a success of Formula 3000. The budget required for Formula One put Grand Prix racing on hold but it occurred to Paul and Jackie that the North American-based Indycar series might be a more viable proposition. Exploratory discussions were held with Roger Penske, a highly successful team owner and leading figure in Indycar circles, as well as Andrew Craig, Ecclestone's equivalent in this smaller branch of the sport, and Dan Rivard, Director of Special Vehicle Operations with the Ford Motor Company in Detroit.

It occurred to Paul and Jackie that the Indycar series might be a more viable proposition

The Stewarts were impressed by the closeness of the racing and the expanding television audience. More than that, however, it was clear that the series had only a handful of truly professional teams. Unlike Formula One, where the quality is more widespread, there was a chance of being competitive – and possibly winning – reasonably quickly in Indycar racing. The Stewarts were giving serious thought to the matter when a damaging internal political war blew up and threatened stability, particularly as the Indianapolis 500, the jewel in the crown of American racing, would be part of a weak breakaway series. Indycar racing without the Indy 500 would be like tennis without Wimbledon. The Stewarts immediately abandoned their tentative plans.

In May 1995, Paul had opened talks with Ford about running its campaign in the British Touring Car Championship, a competitive and high-profile domestic series. It was tempting. But the lure of Formula One was difficult to ignore. In fact, within a matter of weeks it would dominate Paul's thinking.

One of Jackie's regular assignments since retirement had been as television commentator on the Canadian Grand Prix and he duly took up his position with CBC TV in Montreal on 11 June 1995, the day of his fifty-sixth birthday. Stewart would receive a number of gifts but none would have a more profound effect than a suggestion put his way later that night.

He had been continuing his global round of appearances and work for, among others, the Ford Motor Company. He had business to complete in Detroit and he returned from Canada on board a Falcon 900 corporate jet belonging to Ford. Two pairs of comfortably padded seats faced each other, Pullman-style, at the front of the aircraft. Stewart sat in one, to his left sat Bob Rewey (Group Vice-President, Marketing and Sales) and opposite them sat Neil Ressler, Vice-President of Advanced Vehicle Technology for Ford Automotive Operations, and Dan Rivard. Stewart detected that the mood was hardly upbeat.

Ford had been involved in Grand Prix racing since 1967. Their engines had won a hundred and seventy-four Grands Prix and thirteen World Drivers' Championships, three of them with Stewart. No other manufacturer came close to such an impressive tally. There had been bad periods, of course. And this appeared to be one of them.

Ford, in association with Benetton and Michael Schumacher, had won the championship the previous year. It looked good on paper but that success had been a high point in a decade of mediocrity. As if to prove the point, Benetton had ditched Ford in favour of Renault for 1995. Ford's switch to the

Stewart detected that the mood was hardly upbeat

Sauber team was a poor substitute. The Swiss team did not have the experience or the budget enjoyed by Benetton. More important, they did not have Michael Schumacher.

The Canadian Grand Prix had marked the sixth round of the championship and both Sauber-Fords had retired. The best they had to show for their efforts thus far in the season was one fifth and a couple of sixth places, leaving Sauber-Ford a disappointing seventh in the Constructors' Championship. Only once had a Sauber-Ford qualified inside the top ten and there seemed little hope of improvement. Schumacher had already won three races in the Benetton-Renault. That rubbed salt into Ford's wounded image.

'What are we going to do?' asked Ressler.

'You've got to get out,' replied Stewart.

Knowing his subject, and appreciating that this was an informal chat among friends, Stewart did not hold back. He told them that Ford had prevaricated too often. He said Honda and Renault had come into Formula One in recent years and made a huge impression; Peugeot and Mercedes-Benz looked like doing the same. Ford was no longer being taken seriously in the pit lane.

'This is not the way Ford started off in the late sixties,' said Stewart. 'The company was committed then; it was driven. But now I think the fire has gone out. You've talked often enough about quitting Formula One. Now you should do it.'

The men from Ford could see his point, but it was easier said than done. There were too many commitments to Grand Prix racing within marketing and other spheres of the Ford Motor Company.

'In that case,' said Stewart, 'you should stop the bus and rethink your entire strategy. There is no point in carrying on as you are, hoping that a magic wand is going to wave and everything will be OK. It won't.'

'OK,' countered Ressler and Rewey, 'are you interested in putting together a proposal which would represent your views on the best way forward?'

Stewart paused for a second. 'OK,' he said. 'Let me have a think about it.'

The first seeds of the Stewart-Ford Grand Prix team had just been thrown into the wind, five miles above Ontario.

Jackie phoned Paul and told him that Ford was looking for a new direction. Paul needed no second bidding. They set to work immediately. Calling on valuable experience gained while making presentations on behalf of Paul Stewart Racing, an inch-thick dossier was built up over the next few months.

Ford was looking for a new direction. Paul needed no second bidding

No detail was overlooked: the team's goals; the technical input which would be required from Ford; a complete financial breakdown, including salaries for every employee from directors to the odd-job man; costs incurred in the manufacture of the racing car to the purchase price of a delivery van: every nut and bolt was accounted for. But more than that, the report was written in a language its readers would understand and feel comfortable with. Jackie had made sure of that by consulting a business associate he had known for more than twenty-five years.

Here was proof that Jackie's multifarious contacts were priceless at a time like this. When he had signed on with Mark McCormack's International Management Group in 1969 his affairs were handled by Martin Sorrell. Sorrell had since become a multimillionaire and a giant in the advertising business. Part of his empire included J. Walter Thompson. And the Ford Motor Company was one of JWT's major clients. Stewart had no hesitation in calling his former manager.

'We've never done a proposal for this kind of package to a multinational corporation before,' Stewart told Sorrell. 'It isn't that we can't do it. It's just that you only get to do this kind of thing once on such a scale. We know what we need to say, but we want to say it in Ford language. I would like your help.'

Paul Stewart and Rob Armstrong, a New Zealander who had joined PSR as Commercial Director in 1994, flew back and forth to Detroit for discussions with Frank Brooks and Peter Stroh and their team working on the Ford account at JWT. The presentation folder, titled 'A Proposal for Partnership', was gradually knocked into shape in time to meet an appointment with Ford on 30 October.

Paul and Rob took separate flights to America and Paul almost didn't make the rendezvous en route with Jackie at JFK Airport. After sitting on the tarmac at Heathrow for three hours, the flight had to be abandoned. Paul, travelling Economy on the 747, was one of the first off the plane in the dash to the British Airways desk. The only flight available which would make the journey in time was Concorde; a deal was done to allow Paul to fly supersonic to one of the most important meetings of his life. He reached JFK with moments to spare.

Waiting to receive the Stewart party at Ford's World Headquarters in Dearborn were Ressler, Rewey, Rivard, Jac Nasser (Chairman, Ford of Europe), and Bob Transou, the Vice-President of Manufacturing Worldwide. Each member of this small committee had been sent a copy of the proposal in advance. It

A deal was done to allow Paul to fly supersonic to one of the most important meetings of his life

had been presented in an unobtrusive hard-backed three-ring binder carrying the Ford and Paul Stewart Racing logos. The Ford executives, more interested in content rather than a lavish leather binding, had been given the chance to read the document and understand it. This was Stewart's way of saying: 'We're not trying to catch you out; we have no intention of forcing a decision.'

Such an open approach prevailed throughout the presentation. Ford would be welcome to inspect the team's accounts and books at any time. Everything would be straightforward and upfront. The committee was told how much money Stewart would need. The committee said Stewart was not asking for enough, the implication being that the team would be back for more at a later stage. Jackie explained that the figures had been worked out with great care. This was the sum they would require from Ford. The overall budget was realistic and if that proved not to be the case, Stewart – not Ford – would find the difference.

The executives were impressed. Rarely had they been presented a proposal in such a spirit of openness. It had been encapsulated in Jackie Stewart's introductory statement, one which he had constructed carefully since he wanted the words to summarize exactly what he felt the Ford Motor Company required from such a partnership. The opening lines said: 'The Ford Motor Company requires a reliable and trustworthy long-term partner in Formula One'. It was simple but to the point; in many ways it was also a reflection of the fear which Stewart knew many major corporations felt for professional sports.

The Stewart party left the room not knowing the effect of their immaculate presentation. The first indication came six days later when the Ford bosses confirmed that they wanted another meeting. On 6 December, the Stewarts ran through the proposal again. The committee agreed, more or less on the spot, to go ahead.

The Ford Motor Company had made a substantial commitment over a five-year period. Although no figures were mentioned by either party, the media established £100 million as the sum involved, considerably more than the £100,000 which Ford had used to fund its first Grand Prix engine in 1967. Regardless of the precise figure, it was clear that this was a major undertaking. Given the speed of the decision, it was also an endorsement of Stewart's integrity. The seeds of Stewart Grand Prix had now been firmly planted.

High work rate. Catching up with paperwork on board the Stewart executive aircraft.

Non-stop. Jackie spends a typically busy two days in Scotland. After flying in his Jetstream 31 from Northolt to Edinburgh, a drive to his first appointment allows time to catch up on a feature on the team in the American magazine 'Racer'. A meeting with the author of a book on dyslexia is followed by press interviews and a signing session in a major bookstore. Then on to the Highland Spring headquarters at Blackford, near Gleneagles, for a factory tour and discussion with the team's long-time sponsors.

The afternoon is taken up with competition winners and meetings with staff at the Jackie Stewart Shooting School at Gleneagles, with time at the end of the afternoon for a game of golf. A quiet evening is spent in preparation for a busy day of intensive test driving for Jaguar, kicked off by a working breakfast and the recording of comments for a fully detailed report on the car. Then straight to Edinburgh airport and an early-evening flight back to Northolt in readiness for another non-stop day.

Stewart drives again. Jackie uses the golf course to take his mind off business.

CHAPTER TWO

So Little Time

ALMOST TWELVE MONTHS LATER, in November 1996, Paul Stewart was on board another long-haul flight. This time he was travelling east, just about as far from Detroit as it was possible to go. That was not the intention, but it was somehow symbolic. Stewart was a troubled young man.

He was on his way to the Macau Grand Prix, the high point of the Formula Three season and an important event for Paul Stewart Racing. But he was not particularly concerned about that race. The in-flight movie and a pile of reading material held no interest. Neither did the food, despite the blandishments of the attentive cabin crew. He sat, almost in a trance, his mind filled solely with the project which had dominated his every waking hour for the previous year and more.

That was the problem. After all this time, a sudden and potentially devastating sequence of setbacks and financial refusals had placed the Formula One plan in jeopardy. The programme was well advanced. There were more than a hundred people on the Formula One payroll. The launch of the car was imminent. Now Paul and his father had to decide whether or not to axe the entire project. It did not bear thinking about. And the problem was, he could think of nothing else.

The Macau Grand Prix, a dramatic race run on public roads within the tiny Portuguese colony, at least provided a diversion. In the closing stages of the Grand Prix, however, even that looked like unleashing another punch to the stomach and expelling the final puff of Stewart's resistance.

PSR had already won the British Formula Three Championship with Ralph Firman. The twenty-one-year-old Norfolk driver was keen to measure his ability at Macau, an event which would pitch the various national Formula Three champions together, the winner and unofficial Formula Three World Champion being decided on the aggregate result of a two-part race. Paul Stewart recalls the final part.

'Ralph had finished second in the first part. The guy who had won that was out of contention in the second part. So, even though Ralph was not in front, he was winning overall because the race leader, Jarno Trulli, had been too far behind in part one.

'Then, on the last lap, two drivers collide in front of Ralph and hold him up. Trulli is now opening out his lead and eating into the time advantage Ralph had held from the first part. I'm starting to think that we won't win but maybe

Now Paul and his father had to decide whether or not to axe the entire project

we will salvage second or third place. Then Ralph tries to pass the crippled car in front, they collide, and Ralph punctures a tyre. He gets to the hairpin – and crashes. I thought: "I don't believe this!"

'Trulli is heading towards the finish line. He's going to win. Meanwhile, there has been a pile-up and the track is blocked as other cars crash into Ralph. Seconds before Trulli reaches the finishing line, they switch on the red lights to stop the race. The rules say that if a race is stopped, the result is taken from the order at the end of the previous lap. Ralph has won! If Trulli had crossed the finishing line seconds before the red lights appeared – he would have won! It was too much to take in.

'I called my father immediately and told him the result. I have to admit, it was an emotional moment after all the problems we'd been having. It was a very important race to win, seemingly a culmination of everything that had happened during the season. In some respects, it was a gift; in other ways, we had earned it. But it gave me such a boost. It gave me that extra surge of energy which helped me to think positively about everything else.'

Had Stewart been told, when he agreed to the Formula One plan in 1995, that he would need to endure such a traumatic period, he would never have gone ahead. Both Jackie and Paul knew the going would get rough, but once the deal had been agreed with Ford there was no time to speculate on what might happen. They were faced with the here-and-now task of starting a Formula One team from scratch, designing and building a car in twelve months and finding a minimum of £15 million to at least get the team and the car up and running.

The division of responsibilities fell naturally into place. Jackie would use his experience and impeccable contacts to target prospective sponsors; Paul would take care of establishing the team at Milton Keynes. With time in such short supply, it was imperative that they find a technical director straight away. Alan Jenkins was the first choice.

'Contrary to what people might think,' says Paul, 'we didn't have an open chequebook. We had a budget and we had to stick to it. We needed someone who understood that. Alan had worked with the Onyx team when they entered Formula One, more or less on a shoestring by comparison with the budget necessary for Grand Prix racing. Alan had helped hold the whole thing together. But he also had experience of working with top teams such as McLaren in Formula One and Penske in Indycar racing. And we always thought that he

It was imperative that they find a technical director straight away

designed attractive, workmanlike cars. He was working for Arrows at the time and that seemed like a good car too, one which was only short on performance because of the team's limited budget. We talked to several designers but the feeling was that Alan was the man we needed. He had experience which you can't buy.

'We opened discussions. He had other offers but we were very keen to convince him that he should join us. I was very pleased when he said yes. It was a key move, because if we couldn't get a technical director in place early enough then we would have to hire people just to get the project under way and, obviously, that would cause one or two problems when a technical director finally came on board.'

Jenkins was immediately included in discussions with other key personnel, some of whom were already long-standing members of the Paul Stewart Racing operation: David Stubbs, Team Manager; Andy Miller, Technical Team Manager; Colin McGrory, Engineering Manager; Nigel Newton, Financial Controller (later to become Financial Director). Plus, of course, Jackie and Paul Stewart, and Rob Armstrong.

Stewart Grand Prix was inundated with applicants, many of them from front-line teams

One of Paul's first tasks was to book space in the Situations Vacant column of *Autosport*, a half-page advertisement for an aerodynamicist, senior designers, design draughtsmen, and a quality manager appearing in the same issue (11 January 1996) that carried a picture of Jackie on the front cover. The weekly magazine was breaking the news of the Stewart Grand Prix team following a press conference in Detroit on 4 January and one the next day at the Racing Car Show at the Birmingham NEC.

As further advertisements followed, Stewart Grand Prix was inundated with applicants, many of them from front-line teams. Paul and Jackie were able to choose people with experience of Formula One, but while that may have been beneficial in the long run Paul discovered that there were short-term difficulties.

'Obviously, we wanted to make the car as competitive as possible,' says Paul. 'But you can't just give the go-ahead and hope that the money will come in to pay for it. The decisions we made had to be based on the money we had at the time. It was difficult because the people we had taken on board were of a very high calibre. They were accustomed to doing things in a lavish way with established teams which were well funded. We had to get them to pull back and try to understand the situation we were in as a new team.

'It was quite a balancing act. In Alan's case, you don't hire someone with his know-how and then tell him what you want him to do rather than let him do what he believes to be best. There has to be a sensible solution. Alan understood that but it is the natural instinct of a designer or a technician to push the financial people to the limit. They want the best and there is always the thought that maybe the financial people are holding back, being too cautious. Time will eventually show that we allocated everything we could to the car. We didn't actually overspend, which was a success in itself. It suggests that we went about it the right way. We didn't make a loss but there was next to nothing left. It was very tight.'

Money had been spent on reorganizing floor space which had to treble in size. A move to new premises was ruled out because of the disruptive effect it would have on an already tight schedule. Besides, it had been agreed that all available money should be spent on technology.

Initially, it was thought that careful rearranging of the existing premises at 16 Tanners Drive might be sufficient but the spatial demands of a Formula One design and build programme soon became apparent. Fortunately, the very nature of the modern industrial estate on the northern fringe of Milton Keynes worked in their favour. Almost identical premises abutting number 16 became available and the rapidly expanding team more or less burst through the party walls to fill a total of 30,000 square feet. Within six months, you could hardly see the join.

Andy Miller, a linchpin in the racing management structure of PSR since 1989, found himself in the role of unofficial Clerk of Works as the once-pristine workshop turned into a construction site. Miller became an expert in building methods as the truck bay was converted into an air-conditioned drawing office and the Formula Three and Formula Vauxhall race shops were moved two doors down to make way for the Formula One team, plus a carbon fibre area and a pattern shop. The trucks were relocated in Unit 14 (giving access to the Formula One assembly area) and the entire place was rejigged to accept a computer network, plus a telephone system which had expanded from six lines to more than three times as many. Most of the computer installation, incorporating everything from the sophisticated CAD-CAM to an E-mail system, was done at night because the drawing office could not afford the downtime. In the midst of this dust and rubble in 1996, Paul Stewart Racing continued racing and won two championships.

The once-pristine workshop turned into a construction site

'That was important,' says Paul. 'Despite the upheaval and the construction work, we were still winning races, which was a good way of reminding people on the outside that we were still in business, as well as keeping everyone in the team motivated during this disruption. It wasn't easy, but everyone at PSR continued to do a brilliant job.'

Alan Jenkins began his job in an empty room. Before he could produce a car, he had, in close consultation with Paul, to build a design team. They were starting completely from scratch.

'It was more difficult than you might imagine,' says Jenkins. 'Normally, you have something tangible when designing a car. The drawing office is established and the previous year's car provides some form of baseline – good or bad – to work from. Teams usually carry bits over from one car to the next. We were starting from zero and that made the job much bigger.

'The key points were getting the right people on board and setting up the CAD system and then training – or retraining – on how to use it. A deal was struck with EDS Unigraphics. It was more than simply a purchasing arrangement; we were in technical partnership and EDS sent specialists who more or less camped out at the factory while we got up and running. That was a huge issue which had to be taken care of. You find that a lot of time is spent dealing with a great many small points. Then people arrive at different times and need to settle in. They were coming from various teams and differing backgrounds and it was important to give them the chance to express themselves – so you didn't know where that was going to lead! It took two or three months before any sort of broad concept emerged.'

The concept remained broad simply because key issues had yet to be resolved. For instance, Jenkins did not know who would be driving the car. As a result, the cockpit dimensions had to include what he referred to as 'a small comfort zone' to allow the Stewart-Ford to accommodate a driver of above-average height. Similarly, since no decision had been made on which tyre company the team would use, Jenkins knew nothing about the likely tyre compounds and how they might affect items as divergent as suspension design and race/fuel strategy. The specification of the car could not be tied down as much as he would have liked. But there was no time to sit and wait.

While Jenkins and his design team were settling into that windowless open-plan office, which had been designed to have a calming effect with its soft blue lighting and comfortable climate control, Jackie Stewart was facing the

'We were starting from zero and that made the job much bigger'

white heat of commerce in high-powered boardrooms scattered across the globe. He focused on high-technology businesses, on fuel and oil companies, and on financial institutions, mainly in the Far East. For a man with impeccable business manners, Stewart was often nonplussed by a blank refusal to even look at a proposal which offered a business association with the second largest car maker in the world.

'I don't think inept is too strong a word for the business methods of some of these companies,' says Stewart. 'It was quite incredible. If they got in at the ground floor with Ford, the potential for incremental business was enormous. For example, take Ford's telecommunications bill in North America. It runs somewhere between $200 million and $300 million per annum. And what about the link between Ford and mobile phones, both personal and in the car. Who would not want a piece of that? Well, one or two leading names didn't even want a proposal. I was amazed.'

It was the same story with the petrochemical companies and the finance houses. Or most of them anyway. In the face of refusals to be even allowed to state his case, Stewart fell back on his friendship with Sir William Purves, the Chairman of the HSBC Group, one of the world's leading international banking and financial services organizations. Sir William at least took a call from a fellow Scot.

'Why do you want to see me?' he asked Stewart. 'If it's about sponsorship in motor racing, I don't think we are interested.'

'Don't say no without at least hearing what I've got to say,' replied Stewart. Sir William agreed. An appointment was made.

Stewart presented his case to Sir William and Mary Jo Jacobi, the Head of Public Affairs Worldwide for the group. Sir William still had his doubts but he asked Stewart to speak to John Bond, a chief executive officer with the company. Bond knew something about motor racing and he could see the benefits of working with Ford, but even so there were doubts that this was something which the group would consider. Sponsorship in the past had been linked to the arts and to rugby in Hong Kong. It was difficult to imagine the board of a company which included the Hongkong and Shanghai Banking Corporation and the Midland Bank entertaining support for a motor racing team from Milton Keynes.

Sir William promised to raise the matter with the board and if they showed sufficient interest Stewart would be invited to speak, even though such a move

'I don't think inept is too strong a word for the business methods of some of these companies'

would be quite unusual; it was not the sort of thing the board were accustomed to. After hearing from Sir William, the board said they would be prepared to hear Stewart out at 10 a.m. on 28 June 1996. He would be given twenty minutes. Jackie knew he would need to make every second count.

Stewart had spoken in public many times. Nevertheless, he took the trouble to run through his presentation with Kingstree, since the public speaking and presentation consultants would know exactly what was required. On the day before the talk, Stewart asked if he could take a look at the boardroom, an imposing bastion of the financial world with a large and highly polished U-shaped table at its centre. Stewart planned how he could work the room and present the key points he had listed. The board consisted of top businesspeople, chairmen and CEOs from major companies such as Cathay Pacific, Jardine Matheson, Goldman Sachs, and British Airways. They would have no time for flannel or hype. The speech, Stewart estimated, would take fourteen minutes, during which time he would show a four-minute video compiled by his youngest son Mark, a professional and highly competent film producer.

'That's right. You can't get out until you've got an account.'

On the day, the presentation went exactly to plan. Stewart said he would be happy to answer any questions during the few minutes remaining. It was a further twenty-five minutes before the board members had satisfied their curiosity.

Sir William thanked Stewart. He said the board wished to discuss it further – and could he find his way out? Stewart quipped that he had heard it was not an easy place for a man to get out of. To which the CEO of the Midland Bank replied: 'That's right. You can't get out until you've got an account.' Quick as a flash, Stewart said: 'I've got one.' Which he had. With the Midland. That may have been the final touch necessary to secure the deal.

At 3 p.m., Sir William phoned Jackie as promised. He said, quite simply, the board had agreed in principle. They would commit themselves to £25 million over a five-year period.

Stewart was thrilled. This represented a major coup, the first time that a blue-chip company in the financial world had taken such a step. It gave a boost to the continuing search for funds, particularly as Stewart would be shocked when a £60 million deal, agreed the next day, was suddenly withdrawn three weeks later. 'That was a big disappointment – a major kick in the stomach,' recalls Stewart. 'We were talking about title sponsorship. It was very important for everyone concerned. We had shaken hands on the deal and then a brief letter arrived, out of the blue, saying they were withdrawing. I was learning a lot about the way some companies operate in the nineties . . . '

The HSBC deal did much to restore Stewart's faith. He redoubled his efforts as he visited companies such as McDonald's, Mars, and British Telecom. Time was spent in California pursuing Hewlett-Packard in the hope that they would expand on an already successful technical liaison with Paul Stewart Racing.

'Our view was that we could have done a deal with another leading company for the Formula One project,' says Jackie. 'But Hewlett-Packard had been very good to us. They have some top people there – Alex Sozonoff, Vice-President, Sales and Marketing, and Lew Platt, the Chief Executive Officer and Chairman – and we were very keen to maintain the relationship. Hewlett-Packard were obviously going to be around for a long time – and, clearly, that was our intention as well. We had hoped they would come in as full sponsors but the Marketing Director voted against it because it was, in effect, his budget. He wanted to spend the money on other things and we couldn't argue with that.

'However, if Hewlett-Packard couldn't afford to do something with us now, then our feeling was that they might in the future. It was better to give them our support rather than go off with someone else. In the end, they agreed to be a supplier to Stewart Grand Prix in a deal which was very favourable to us. We were delighted to maintain the relationship.'

The strongest link of all continued to be with the Ford Motor Company, but even then, the Stewarts had to direct their attention towards a growing concern as the summer of 1996 headed towards autumn. Ford's link with the engine builders, Cosworth Engineering in Northampton, had been established for more than thirty years. While having total respect for the engineering talent at Cosworth, Jackie Stewart felt that they needed help to change their culture and technology to bring the company into line as Formula One raced towards the millennium. Cosworth is owned by Vickers. Not only did Stewart spend time and effort to get to see the chairman, he also chased Ford.

'It's a Ford engine and it's their commitment,' said Stewart. 'Ford had to put more technology into Cosworth and apply more pressure to the British company than they had ever done before. I had to stress that point continually. I wasn't very popular because of that but we had to get the job done. At the end of the day, the Ford Motor Company was not doing this because they

'I wasn't very popular because of that but we had to get the job done'

expected me to be a nice guy. I had to bring them a winning combination. To do that, we would be dependent on a number of people. One of the major players was Cosworth. We had to make it work.'

Stewart had signed an exclusive deal to use the Ford Zetec-R V10 in 1997. This was a new engine, the first ten-cylinder from Cosworth, and one which had been introduced at the start of the 1996 season. Ford had a contract with Sauber and the Swiss team had not been pleased when they learned that the engine which they would spend twelve months sorting out would then go to Stewart.

Sauber made strenuous efforts to gain access to the V10 in 1997. When it was made clear that they could not have parity with Stewart, the suggestion arose that they might have an engine that would always be two stages of development behind the V10 used by Stewart. Either way, Stewart was not happy about any form of power sharing. He felt that Ford and Cosworth would have enough on their plate developing and building sufficient engines for Stewart Grand Prix without having to worry about supplying someone else.

This was not a reflection on the ability of Ford and Cosworth. History had shown that engine manufacturers such as Honda, Mercedes-Benz, and Peugeot favoured supplying a single team – at least until they were capable of providing a seriously competitive engine which could win races as a matter of course. But the suggestion of supplying Sauber remained. In the end, Stewart had to go all the way to senior management at Ford to explain that the massive commitment and effort being put in by Ford, Cosworth, and Stewart Grand Prix would be heavily diluted by a decision to supply another team. They agreed. But Jackie Stewart was not popular in certain quarters of the Formula One paddock.

Not that he cared too much about that. Besides, there were equally pressing matters emerging as the months slipped by. The deal with HSBC was formally announced on 17 September. Jackie, meanwhile, had approached a respected business contact, Tan Sri Arumugam, and reopened discussions with his friends in Malaysia. If they could not support an entire team, it made sense to at least be involved in Formula One given that Malaysia was intending to host a Grand Prix in 1998. On 26 November, Stewart flew to Kuala Lumpur for the Prime Minister's formal announcement that the Stewart Grand Prix car would carry a 'Visit Malaysia' emblem on a prominent position on the front and rear wings. Again, this was a unique deal in motor sport terms, one which

This was a unique deal in motor sport terms, one which had come about through Stewart's personal contacts

had come about through Stewart's professionalism, persistence, and personal contacts.

The actual launch of the car was only a matter of weeks away and, as yet, not all the budget was in place. But if Jackie and Paul had thought that was bad, they were about to be plunged into a crisis on a day, less than a week before the launch, which will for ever be known as Black Friday.

'There had been ups and downs during the year; you expect that,' says Paul Stewart. 'But this was something else again. It was a day when we were expecting certain key decisions – and they all went sour. One after the other. Time was running out.

'Rob Armstrong, Nigel Newton, and I gathered in my father's office. It was agreed that we needed to go over old territory, approach people who had already said no and try and persuade them, push them along. It was a very difficult day. And while all that was going on, we had to make sure it did not affect morale within the team. You can't be dishonest with people, but at the same time you don't want to cause unnecessary anxiety. You don't want them to become frightened, in case they see an advertisement for another job and suddenly jump ship. It had taken time to build up a team of very good people of whom we were very proud. We didn't want to lose them. All told, it was a stressful time in my father's office that afternoon.'

It was also pretty fraught in the technical offices downstairs. If the commercial side of the team had been having its setbacks, life had not been plain sailing with the car itself, the focal point of the entire team and the item which was consuming most of the money in the first place.

ABOVE. Alan Jenkins: Technical Director and quiet man behind all the noise.

RIGHT. Out of our hands now. Team Manager David Stubbs (right) and Stewart-Ford crew members wait for the cars to return from the track.

BELOW: Giving HSBC a place in the sun.

RIGHT. Through the look-in glass. Beyond a glazed partition in the office suite Jackie, Nigel Newton (Financial Director), Rob Armstrong (Commercial Director) and Paul hold a high-level discussion. BELOW. Not a drawing board in sight. Alan Jenkins at his computer-dominated workplace.

LEFT. Full flow. Head of Aerodynamics, Eghbal Hamidy (right), and Pete Sumner get down to a detailed study.

BELOW. Clerk of Works. As Technical Coordinator, Andy Miller had more than just the building of cars to worry about during the reconstruction of the factory.

Clear air and a clear head. Paul gets away from it all high above Villars in Switzerland, the country where he spent most of his youth.

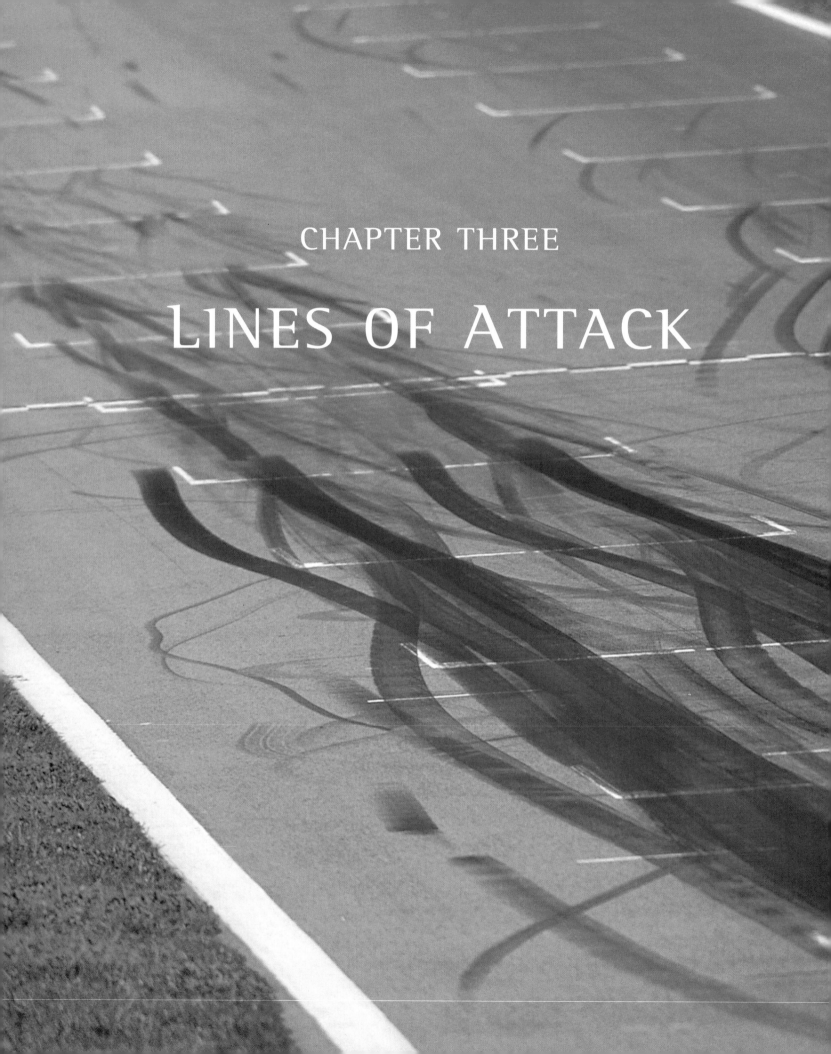

CHAPTER THREE

LINES OF ATTACK

ON THE DAY that Rubens Barrichello qualified his Jordan-Peugeot on the front row for the 1996 Brazilian Grand Prix, Alan Jenkins was beginning the initial layout of the car Barrichello would race in his home Grand Prix a year later. The connection had not been made on 30 March 1996; indeed, the choice of drivers was some way down the list of priorities. Of more immediate concern was getting down to detail design work on the car and organizing its manufacture. In that respect, there were two very important points of principle which Jenkins wanted to establish if this car was to have any worthwhile performance advantage over the opposition.

The rules clearly define the dimensions of Formula One cars, thus closing down the scope for adventurous and pioneering design work in search of making a faster and more efficient machine. Any gains would be very small and largely through detailed study of the aerodynamics. To that end Jenkins, in company with Eghbal Hamidy, argued in favour of building a half-size wind tunnel model of the car. It was something which Jenkins knew Hamidy would need if the Head of Aerodynamics was to exercise his considerable skills. That was Jenkins's first aim. The second was to promote the idea of having the chassis built in-house instead of becoming locked into the schedules imposed by an outside firm.

These were two major issues for a fledgeling team to consider. Few restraints had been placed on Jenkins when it came to designing the car. He had been given a reasonable budget, one which was neither excessive nor a serious handicap, with the instruction to use suitable outside suppliers where possible and avoid spending money on lavishly equipping the factory at this stage. The bottom line was to have the car ready for the launch in early December.

Jenkins had no complaints. But he and Hamidy, a former aerodynamicist with Williams, were as insistent as they could be on the question of the half-size model, the kind of tool to which only Williams and Ferrari had access. It would cost £200,000 to make. But that would not be the half of it in terms of logistics and finance. There were very few half-size wind tunnels in the world. One of the best was at Swift Engineering in San Clemente, California, a facility which, apart from the obvious long-distance expense, would cost £3,000 a day. The Williams team had made use of it while their tunnel was being shifted as the world champions moved premises in the winter and spring of 1996.

It would cost £200,000 to make. But that would not be the half of it in terms of logistics and finance

Stewart decided to bite the bullet. The tunnel would be free from 1 July and the design team, the recruitment for which had been completed a month before, worked with that in mind. By 8 August, the chassis shape had been finalized. Construction of the first patterns began the next day, the process being aided enormously by the complex computer technology which had been installed in Milton Keynes.

Stewart's Information Technology expert, Steve Nevey, became a key player in a company which had committed itself to using computer-aided design (CAD). There would not be a drawing board in the place, this being the first time that a Grand Prix car had been designed completely on a screen. Stewart immediately formed a strong partnership with EDS, which provided the Unigraphics CAD software system and then continued to monitor progress, updating and altering the system to suit the team's requirements as they became more detailed and precise.

Similarly, Hewlett-Packard went beyond the mere supply of computer hardware, the company with a £26 billion turnover becoming involved in discussions on the latest developments within the team. And EDS, through MSC, a computer division specializing in stress-analysis tests on newly designed components, threw itself into the challenging and intensive task of producing a Formula One car. The flexibility and scope of the CAD system was such that everyone associated with the design process could work off the same database. This was particularly useful for Egbhal Hamidy in California, where connection by modem to the system allowed the aerodynamicist to use the wind tunnel to instantly check the effect of any updates and changes made in the design office.

Having said that, Jenkins and his team actually managed to reduce expensive time in the wind tunnel thanks to their technical liaison with Ford. The association between the two companies went beyond the supply of engines, Ford's advanced resources giving the Stewart design team extensive experience with Computational Fluid Dynamics (CFD). In simple terms, this allowed the use of computer software as a faster and cheaper substitute for the wind tunnel when it came to addressing a number of key aerodynamic issues relating to the car.

Specialists from Ford's Advanced Vehicle Technology Division (AVT) also helped to produce the integrated electrics system and electronics package. Similarly, access to a RAMSIS computer program gave the team the opportunity to

There would not be a drawing board in the place, this being the first time that a Grand Prix car had been designed completely on a screen

apply three-dimensional modelling techniques to the cockpit of the SF-1, thus making this the first chassis to be designed from the inside out. Now all they had to do was build it.

Jenkins had been keen on making the carbon fibre chassis, or tub as it is known, in-house. It seemed a bit of a forlorn hope since the manufacturing process calls for a massive cylindrical pressurized oven (an autoclave) in which the chassis is baked. There was no way the team could even contemplate the capital expenditure required. Besides, there was nowhere to put it even if they could afford the necessary £120,000. Then Jenkins remembered an autoclave installed by Yamaha and now redundant in premises less than a mile away. It was too good an opportunity to miss.

'Building the chassis ourselves was to be an enormous advantage,' says Jenkins. 'It meant we could react to small subtle issues that continually arose as the design proceeded.'

Jenkins had his hands full as he coordinated the project, literally ensuring the components fitted together like hand and glove. While the engineers at Cosworth worked on the installation of the V10 engine, Jenkins was in close discussion with Xtrac, the manufacturers of the six-speed gearbox which would hang off the back of the engine and carry the rear suspension and wing as well as a crash structure designed to absorb a rear impact.

The crash box was a new addition to the mandatory safety features necessary to withstand a rigorous series of crash tests. Before the SF-1 could be declared fit for racing by the sport's governing body, the FIA, the chassis would be subjected to a ferocious series of impact tests in laboratory conditions. The Stewart-Ford eventually gained a clean bill of health, but not before a routine failure, which was part of the learning curve, was interpreted as some sort of terminal disaster by uninformed sources outside the team. But first the car had to be made ready in time for the launch, originally scheduled for 18 December but moved forward eight days, thus providing another turn of the screw for the production team, already working flat out.

When he wasn't in discussion with his father over finance, Paul Stewart was taking care of the details which to some would appear minor, but to the Stewarts would give the team that extra edge. Jackie's reputation for remembering the importance of the minutiae had been enhanced when he insisted that each time the Paul Stewart Racing transporter was parked in a paddock, it should be jacked up and the wheels positioned to allow the tyre manufacturer's name to be aligned at the top of each wheel. Nit picking? 'No,' said Stewart. 'It's a matter of pride. If the truck driver bothers to get that right, I can guarantee he's looking after the important things.'

It was part of the presentation creed which Jackie carried with him to every branch of his business. When working on the forecourt of his father's garage in Dumbuck, Jackie made sure the service bay was the cleanest in Dumbartonshire. Thirty years later, it was not uncommon to see him removing litter from the team's garage area or pulling weeds at his shooting school in Gleneagles. Now it would be the same with the Formula One team. No detail would be too small to ignore.

A great deal of thought had gone into the steering wheel, one which was made in-house rather than relying on the traditional manufacturers. These days, the wheel does more than simply point the car in the right direction. It is a central control unit, a hands-on command device from where, by a series of levers behind the spokes, the driver can change up and down through the gearbox and operate the clutch. Various buttons operate the radio, the rear light (for use in poor visibility), the selection of neutral, and the operation of the rev-limiter which is necessary to keep the car below a predetermined pace when obeying the speed limit in the pit lane during the race.

It is a central control unit, a hands-on command device

Rather than adopt a circular shape, the top of the wheel would be flattened in order to prevent the rim from protruding above the cockpit; an aerodynamic consideration as well as improving the view for the driver from his deeply reclining position. The straight section of the rim would also house the digital readout, the various parameters being controlled from yet another button on the steering wheel boss.

If the wheel was to be, as it were, bespoke, then why not go the whole hog and choose a colour to match the team's identity? Paul selected a shade of blue for the suede, with white stitching neatly completing the Scottish national colours. But just who would get to lay their hands on this neatly crafted piece of kit?

On 13 May, Paul and Jackie had opened discussions with Jan Magnussen. There was no need for a formal introduction since they knew each other well, the Dane having established a record when he won fourteen out of eighteen races on his way to the 1994 British Formula Three Championship with PSR. Since then he had driven once for McLaren in Formula One – as a late substitute when Mika Hakkinen suffered from appendicitis – and finished tenth in the 1995 Pacific Grand Prix at Aida in Japan. The three-time World Karting Champion had impressed everyone with his maturity and intelligence in what was considered to be a very difficult car, but since then his career appeared to have gone on hold as he drove touring cars, without much success, for Mercedes-Benz in Europe. For the Stewarts, however, Magnussen was the ideal choice, Jackie claiming: 'Jan has as much talent in a racing car as I've ever seen – with as good a head as anybody I've ever seen in this sport.' With such a glowing endorsement, it was scarcely a surprise when, on 3 October, the details were finalized and Magnussen signed a four-year deal.

By now, Jackie and Paul had become the focus of intensifying media attention as magazines prepared features in advance of the launch and newspapers ran stories on the unique nature of this family alliance. On Monday 2 September, the *Daily Telegraph* carried a profile on Paul, the text speculating on the identity of his drivers. By coincidence, one of the biggest sports stories of the season was splashed across the front of the same newspaper: in a shock move, Damon Hill was going to be kicked out by Frank Williams at the end of the season.

Straight away, the champion-elect was seen as a likely candidate for Stewart. On 18 September Jackie and Paul flew to Dublin to meet Damon and his lawyer, Michael Breen. Four days later, in the paddock at Estoril, they talked with Rubens Barrichello and his manager, Geraldo Rodrigues, for a second time, the discussions with the Brazilians having been opened at the Belgian Grand Prix four weeks before.

There were mixed feelings about taking Hill on board since his presence, while being enormously advantageous for all the obvious reasons, would also create huge pressure which the team did not need in its first year. In the end, Hill signed for Arrows and on 22 October the Stewarts were delighted to have Barrichello's signature on a three-year agreement, Paul possessing a particularly useful insight thanks to having competed against Rubens when they raced in Formula 3000.

It was another shrewd move. They had caught the Brazilian on the start of an upswing from a period of disenchantment. He had made his Formula One debut with Jordan and stayed with them for four years, which was perhaps one season too many, the team had been struggling, and Barrichello's motivation had suffered. He appeared to be going nowhere and yet he knew he had much to offer. Despite having sixty-four Grands Prix under his belt,

Jackie and Paul flew to Dublin to meet Damon and his lawyer, Michael Breen

he was only twenty-four, a youngster in Formula One terms. He was the perfect man to fly Stewart's colours – which was another detail which needed attending to as the launch date closed in.

The choice of colour scheme for the Stewart-Ford was made difficult by the fact that with less than a month to go before the unveiling the livery designers could not work on the car simply because it was still in pieces. Templates had to be taken from the half-size wind tunnel model and even that was fraught with difficulty because the model was only available for this work between nine at night and four the next morning.

Central to the livery would be a splash of tartan, the Stewart trademark ever since Jackie had decorated his crash helmet with a band of Royal Stewart tartan soon after he started racing in the early sixties. Jackie wore tartan caps, a habit which he extended to his mechanics when racing for BRM and Tyrrell. He even went as far as having the seat of his racing car covered in the predominantly red material.

When Paul began racing, he followed a similar theme by choosing the Hunting Stewart tartan for his helmet. It seemed logical to commission a new tartan by combining the Royal and the Hunting Stewarts. In March 1996, The Scottish Tartan Society registered a hybrid, to be known as Racing Stewart. Having been established before the Stewarts had even thought of going into Formula One, it was natural that this should form a major part of the symbolism for the team.

The base colour on the car would be white, chosen for its visibility on tele-vision and the ability to highlight sponsor identification without clashing with the various corporate colours. But this would not be any old splash of white. The team deliberately selected a soft shade, one which would not glare on camera. The tartan was also incorporated in the team logo, designed by Carter Wong & Partners, the London-based company which had carried out work for the FIA and major industrial concerns. The pointed end of the logo matched the lines on the front of the car when viewed from the side, the tail adding to the logo as a twist in the design completed the effect of movement. It was a simple but instantly recognizable design which would work comfortably with the traditional blue oval Ford badge. Now they simply needed to be fixed to the car. Easier said than done. As Monday 9 December drew to a close, the SF-1 was still in bits as the midnight oil burned more fiercely than ever in Tanners Drive.

ABOVE, TOP. Been there and done it. Magnussen's boss offers timely advice and observations.

ABOVE. Rubens thrived in his new environment, rising to the challenge after learning the F1 ropes with Jordan.

OPPOSITE. The steering wheel on the SF-1 does more than simply point the car in the right direction. The top two paddles change gear (left for down-shifting; right for changing up); the bottom paddles, which are linked, operate the clutch. The red flick-switch (top left) operates the radio. The yellow button (top right) brings in the rev limiter to ensure the pit lane speed restriction is adhered to. The white button, planned for a future function, served no purpose during 1997 but the five-stop click switch (bottom right) controls the engine mapping selection to suit differing track conditions. The blue button selects the dashboard display while the yellow puts the gearbox into neutral.

OPPOSITE. The clean and efficient lines of the Stewart-Ford are clearly defined.

LEFT. Rubber newcomer. Bridgestone played a vital part in the first year for both the tyre company and Stewart-Ford.

BELOW. The hefty seat harness keeps the driver firmly in place while experiencing as much as 3.5 G under braking.

CHAPTER FOUR

FLESH AND BLOOD

ALAN JENKINS DID NOT SEE HIS CAR with its wheels in place until five o'clock on the morning of the launch. It was the first time in nine months that he had been able to step back and assess the team's creation as a whole. Up until that point the car, code-named SF-1, had been a project, then a series of images on a screen, then a model and a disparate collection of parts. Now, at last, it had all come together on the factory floor. It mattered little what time of day it was.

Jenkins found he was not alone. At a rough estimate, fifty members of the team had materialized in the workshop even though half of them had no need to be there. This was the moment – the first of many important milestones – that Stewart Grand Prix had been working flat out towards. No way were they going to miss this.

A feeling of expectation and satisfaction went through the room. People smiled. Cameras clicked. Not a lot was said. There was no need. The white racer with its tartan flashes was an eloquent summary of the intense effort; a fitting climax to nine months' labour. Jenkins described the atmosphere as: 'Just great. A brilliant moment.'

Until this point, there had been no need to have the car complete, all four wheels in place. It hadn't been going anywhere. Now it was. And quickly. The car was rolled into a waiting truck, the crew anxious to reach the Marriott Hotel in London's Grosvenor Square before the morning rush. Once there, they would need to park, probably in a forbidden zone, unload and manhandle their precious cargo into a function room, the entrance of which had not been designed to accept such an awkward item. These things took time. The earlier it could be done, the better. Certainly, they wanted to be finished before traffic wardens, irascible commuters, and curious hotel guests were too much in evidence.

The truck arrived at 7 a.m. The operation went like clockwork, and the car was through the doors, onto ramps, and in place on a prepared stage with no difficulty at all. There were five hours before the unveiling in front of the world's press. There was much to be done.

By 9 a.m. the busy but narrow hotel foyer seemed to be overrun by besuited men with tartan ties, earpieces, microphones, and preoccupied expressions. Some were from Ford, some from Stewart Grand Prix. All were checking and double-checking schedules and plans. Their neat, businesslike appearance

**This was the moment
Stewart Grand Prix
had been working
flat out towards**

belied the organized chaos in the large room beyond the walnut double doors.

The car was the only thing at rest. Banging and hammering signalled the completion of a photographers' and television gallery. Construction men in jeans and sweatshirts studied a detailed plan illustrating the stage and the precise position of an overhead gantry carrying twenty-six lights of various strengths and hues. A massive curving picture, showing an empty starting grid at Melbourne, scene of the first race in three months' time, provided a clever backdrop. A control centre was being established behind an equally temporary screen. And more men in suits dashed hither and thither, speaking earnestly into walkie-talkies and mobile phones. The once-spacious room, with its high ceiling and windowless walls, was already putting the air-conditioning to the test. So much to be done and so little time.

By 10 a.m. Jackie, immaculate as ever, had been in and out several times, always with someone in tow. Paul, in an open-neck shirt and sweater, had made a more relaxed entrance but the time had come for father and son to return to their rooms and change into the more formal tartan kilts for what was becoming a noticeably Scottish affair.

The master of ceremonies would be Dougie Donnelly, the gentle Celtic burr of the BBC TV sports presenter fitting the occasion and sounding even more appropriate as a piper reported for duty. Apart from the highlights on the car, the driving seat had been covered with Racing Stewart tartan. At the back of the SF-1, long, narrow strips of tartan cloth served a more practical purpose as they hid important details of the aerodynamics on the undertray. These complex features had been evolved after many hours in the wind tunnel. They would be seen eventually, of course. But the longer the eyes of the competition could be diverted from the Stewart solution, the better. In any case, some of the detailed work on the transmission was not quite complete and some eagle-eyed anorak would be sure to spot it. Eghbal Hamidy had suggested some form of cover. Using the tartan in this way was the idea of Iain Cunningham, a former Williams employee and a seasoned campaigner in racing car launches. And a Scot, to boot.

By 10.45 a.m. Barrichello and Magnussen had arrived. The drivers sat quietly in the background, for once minor players on a stage dominated by their car. Jackie and Paul were dressed for action. Well, almost. Paul, unaccustomed to such formality early in the day, had accidentally put on his dress evening shoes. A swift change to the morning footwear took place before he

Narrow strips of tartan cloth hid important details of the aerodynamics on the undertray

began pacing the floor, speech in hand. Jackie, meanwhile, was at the podium, reading his lines, his voice drowned by the clatter of activity and the increasing buzz of conversation.

'Quiet, please!' A producer from the communications company in charge of the sound system called for silence at 11 a.m., the scheduled time for the one and only rehearsal. Helen, dressed in a charcoal-grey suit, slipped gracefully into the room and was immediately embraced by Mark as he prepared for more video work. Jackie, busy now with the seating plan for the VIP guests, found Barrichello and Magnussen and called them onto the stage. Straightening their tartan ties, he briefed his drivers on their movements. They looked awkward and ill-at-ease in plain grey suits.

The rehearsal finally got under way in shortened form as Donnelly bade everyone welcome, each speaker then stepping up to the microphone, reading the first line of their speech, and calling the next person forward. With the running order established, attention was paid to the sequence in which photographs would be taken. Masterminded by Steve Madincea of Prism, the marketing company in charge of coordinating many of Ford's motor sport programmes, the Stewarts and their drivers worked out where to sit and stand, and which direction to face when the turntable stage had swivelled once more to show the car at a different angle. It seemed a tricky enough manoeuvre as the clock ticked and the pressure began to mount. Behind the partition screening off the rear quarter of the room a buzz of conversation was imperceptibly rising to a babble as the media signed in and kick-started their day by the table loaded with coffee.

Throughout the serious preparations in the auditorium, this remained very much a family occasion. As Helen helped Jackie with a touch of facial cream, Paul's wife Victoria arrived with their son Dylan. The two-year-old was hiked onto the stage and into the cockpit of the car for an informal photograph. Twenty-nine years before, during a private test session at Oulton Park, Jackie had done exactly the same thing with two-year-old Paul for the benefit of a photographer from the *Daily Express* before taking the Matra Formula Two car onto the Cheshire track. This was in the early days of Jackie's career, before he had won a World Championship. A lot had changed since then. Any yet, in some respects, nothing had changed at all.

Very little changes when it comes to the methods of the media. By 11.45 a.m. the reception room was full to bursting, an impressive turnout of

They looked awkward and ill-at-ease in plain grey suits

journalists and photographers from abroad indicating the power of the Stewart name in Formula One. As a reminder, the walls were lined with poignant black and white photographs of Jackie in action as a racing driver, the Racing Stewart background drapes bringing the focus up to date.

For the motor racing hack, the launch of a new car becomes a matter of routine, a time to catch up on gossip with colleagues rather than listen to the familiar enthusiastic platitudes issuing from the speaker's platform. 'This is the best car we have ever made . . . eight per cent faster than last year's car . . . new drivers bring new hope . . . delighted to welcome our latest sponsors . . . we have high hopes of regularly scoring points.' The journalists have heard it all before. Far better to find out who's doing what to whom elsewhere in the motor racing firmament.

The chat in the Marriott on 10 December covered speculation that Nigel Mansell might make yet another Formula One comeback with Jordan. There was the story that Benetton's Technical Director was joining Ferrari and the Williams designer, who wanted to leave, was being forced to stay. And yet most conversations carried a familiar theme: a genuine interest in the Stewart Grand Prix car. Had anyone seen it yet? Was it radical? Was the team ready? Would they cut the mustard? Had they found enough money to do the job properly?

Clearly, much was at stake here. Anyone who thought this might be a run-of-the-mill launch had that finally dispelled at 11.50 a.m. when the partition rolled back and the distinctive skirl of the lone piper filled the room beyond. It was time to get down to business.

The venue had been chosen with a view to accommodating a reasonable turnout. Stewart Grand Prix had undervalued themselves. Everyone of note in the motor sport media was there. The seating was quickly filled, tardy members of the press finding themselves standing shoulder to shoulder in the aisles. The VIP guests representing Ford and the sponsors made their way to the reserved seats. Seventeen cameramen took focus from the television platform as Jackie Stewart led his party into the room and the background music rose to a crescendo. At 12.09 p.m., Dougie Donnelly stepped up to the lectern. The build-up had been perfectly executed. Everyone was raring to go.

Donnelly spent two minutes outlining the programme for the launch and delivering 'housekeeping notes' which ranged from how and when the photographs could be taken, to a plea for everyone present to switch off their

The distinctive skirl of the lone piper filled the room beyond: it was time to get down to business

mobile phones. It was a reasonable request, which initiated a fair bit of fumbling among the packed audience. Then he called forward Martin Whitaker, the Director of European Motorsport for the Ford Motor Company.

In common with many present in the room, Whitaker was doing battle with the stubborn remnants of a winter cold. But he got his message across. Ford had been in Formula One for thirty years; Jackie Stewart remained the most successful Ford-powered Grand Prix driver of all time; the link between the two was logical. Whitaker then stressed that sentiment had no part in the decision. The association with Formula One was good for engineering advancement within Ford as a whole and, in turn, the automotive giant was going to lend the power of its technology to Stewart's team. It would be the biggest effort yet by Ford. 'I'll tell you this now,' concluded Whitaker. 'We have a clear objective with this programme: to help Stewart-Ford become FIA Formula One World Champions.' Brave talk.

Whitaker made way for Jackie Stewart. He scanned the room and bade welcome to what he referred to as 'an army' of media. He spoke as if this had been an impromptu reaction to the massive turnout. In fact, it had been part of the original script but its delivery bore all the hallmarks of a polished public speaker. And yet, for once, the odd stumble here and there gave the only hint of the importance of this occasion to John Young Stewart.

No one envied Paul. Following Jackie had to be the most difficult task imaginable

Forget the three world championships and twenty-seven victories. He was embarking on a mission which would provide a test even more severe than anything he had endured while racing. He described it as 'the most daunting challenge I have ever faced'. A reputation as one of the most skilled performers of the last thirty years would not begin to shore up his team should it show signs of failing. But there was no going back now.

Professional as ever, Stewart made mention of the sponsors and laid heavy emphasis on the partnership with Ford. Then he knocked rumours on the head by stressing that the team was fully equipped and fully funded, ready to go. And, he was pleased to say, there was still space to sell on the side of the car. Normally, that is a matter of regret at a car launch since it indicates a budget which is incomplete. Stewart's upbeat speech was impressive. He was centre stage for thirteen minutes, entirely at ease towards the end. At 12.30 p.m., he handed over to his elder boy.

No one envied Paul. Following Jackie had to be the most difficult task imaginable, particularly for a son who was naturally in awe of his father's achievements. But the Managing Director of Stewart Grand Prix bent his mind to the task, outlining the work that had been done, stressing that this was the first Formula One car to be designed from scratch by computer and reminding the audience that this was the first 1997 Formula One car to be unveiled. Paul explained that Stewart Grand Prix had gathered together a hundred and one people in a short space of time and the result of their efforts was under the tartan drape behind him.

In the midst of the excitement, it was easy to overlook the toll this had taken on Paul Stewart. The task of making it all actually happen had fallen to him and this was the crowning achievement in the opening phase of a long campaign. In nine months, Stewart Grand Prix had gone from a line on a computer to a 200 m.p.h. Formula One car. And now the world's media were gathered here to see it. It was a poignant moment. As Paul tried to express his feelings and the pride which came from witnessing the first fruits of such a thrilling project, he could see, out of the corner of his eye, his father and mother, his brother Mark, and his wife Victoria as she did her best to keep Dylan amused. More than anything, this emphasized the family element which ran through the entire venture. When Paul reached the point in his notes which referred to thanking his father, the sensation became overwhelming. He suffered a speaker's worst nightmare and literally became choked with emotion. As he clutched his chest and faltered, the entire room felt for him.

Paul glanced towards his father – and saw that he was close to tears. There was nothing for it but to press on. Gathering his thoughts in the endless seconds which followed, Paul composed himself and said: 'From the bottom of my heart, I'd like to thank my father for this tremendous opportunity. I've waited so long for this moment.' When he called his father onto the stage to help unveil the car, Jackie's first move was to give Paul a warm embrace. It was a generous gesture, unimpeded by pride on such a public platform. Many in the audience felt Jackie had also acted on their behalf.

At 12.40 p.m. the Racing Stewart tartan cover was removed, the white paintwork gleaming under the bank of spotlights. Synthesized music played and the stage rotated through 360°. The room was a blitz of flashlights. Those seated in the front rows stood up to get a better view. The domino effect had everyone on their feet, much to the obvious despair of the cameramen in the gallery beyond. The drivers, having been introduced by Jackie during his speech, were called onto the stage once more for the benefit of the

He suffered a speaker's worst nightmare and literally became choked with emotion

photographers who, as usual, had ignored all instructions and were hogging the outer edge. By now the television crews were roaring their displeasure, but to no obvious effect. The Stewart Grand Prix bandwagon was well and truly rolling. There was the clear impression that nothing would stop it now.

As Dougie Donnelly asked everyone to stand back and allow the television crews to film a repeat of the unveiling – or the 'reveal', to use television-speak – the photographers merely intensified their elbowing and jostling as the rest of the Stewart family joined Jackie and Paul on stage. It was perfect 'lifestyle' material, the Stewart motor racing dynasty revealed naturally and in an atmosphere of warmth and good humour. It was hard to imagine any other Formula One team putting such a human face on the launch of a racing car.

Standing quietly to one side, Rob Armstrong breathed a sigh of relief as he surveyed the car and, in particular, the sponsorship logos. Only he knew the struggle it had taken to get two of them there. Texaco had been a late and very welcome addition but the Commercial Director was looking in particular at the identification for Sanyo. In his briefcase, Armstrong had the official paperwork. No problems there – except that he had been up all night thrashing out the final details, a signature on the Sanyo contract arriving by fax at the Stewart headquarters at 4 a.m. By then, the go-ahead had been given to fix the logos to the car; time was pressing and departure for London was imminent. 'It was a gamble we had to take,' said Armstrong 'If necessary, I would have removed the logos by blowtorch at the last minute!'

He had the signature – but that was not the end of the story. It was necessary to receive a guarantee from the parent company before the deal could be officially sealed. Rob rushed home, slept for an hour, and then headed for London. The necessary guarantee from Sanyo arrived at the Marriott by messenger at 10 a.m., two hours before the car – and its logos – were due to be unveiled.

'In some ways,' he said, glancing round the room, 'getting this far has been like removing the Sword of Damocles. But there is no doubt that having the date of the launch hanging over us did provide a pressure point, not just for the team, but for our prospective sponsors as well. It focused everyone on finalizing the deals. It's a huge relief now that everything is in place.'

The hard work was over in certain respects, but for Jackie it had scarcely begun. Each leading member of the team had been allocated a 'minder' from

'If necessary, I would have removed the logos by blowtorch at the last minute!'

the Ford Motor Company in order to process the requests for interviews. Huddles of reporters were dotted around the room as Jackie, Paul, Alan Jenkins, Martin Whitaker, and the drivers spoke into tape-recorders and faced cameras.

Jackie was the most popular, Stuart Dyble from Ford's Public Affairs office having his work cut out to keep the media satisfied. Stewart did not stop talking for two hours. He began by doing a live piece from the edge of the stage, straight into the BBC Radio 5 Live *One O'clock News*, the sports producer Gill Pulsford being impressed by Stewart's utterly calm demeanour and fluent answers in the midst of the controlled chaos around him. Then he was off, saying it all again for another radio station.

He finished just after 3 p.m., sitting on the edge of the stage, swigging from a bottle of Highland Spring, and chatting as if this was the first interview of the day. He was with Alan Henry of *Autocar* and Heinz Prueller from Austria, motor sport journalists who had dealt with Stewart when he was a racing driver and knew him well. Both could appreciate the significance of the day and what it meant to the former champion.

'Paul's speech. That must have been a strong moment for you,' said Prueller quietly.

'Yes, Heinz,' replied Stewart. 'It was a strong moment for me and it was a strong moment for Paul. Keep in mind that I have been round this merry-go-round lots of times. I've done this before. I've had all kinds of media attention but I've never seen a media launch as big as this. For a young man to face that after working so hard for so many months – a lot of pressure and strain – he was very good to be able to carry it off like that. I know how difficult it is. I also know that without Paul I could not have done this. I'm really very happy to have him here.'

Henry shifted the emphasis onto more controversial ground by asking Stewart about his drivers. Referring to Barrichello's latent talent, the man from *Autocar* and the *Guardian* wondered if Stewart could succeed where Jordan had failed.

'I don't think Eddie Jordan failed,' came the tactful response as Jackie refused to rise to the bait. 'I think he did a very good job for Rubens and allowed him to get a very good start to his career and gain valuable experience. But I think that I probably understand what a Grand Prix driver needs better than most team owners. It's different if you have been in the forefront

'I've done this before. I've had all kinds of media attention but I've never seen a media launch as big as this'

and can understand what it feels like to have certain inadequacies – which we all have – and to suffer disappointment. It isn't easy to bring everything together in order to be a successful Formula One driver. If it's not handled carefully, it can go wrong. I honestly believe Rubens will really be assisted by this team.'

At an opportune moment, Stewart did not fail to mention a sponsor or two. He slipped easily into his patter, mentioning HSBC as a good example of the business opportunities created for the team's partners. He made it sound like it was a one-way street – with Stewart Grand Prix doing the sponsors a favour.

'The biggest thing for us,' said Stewart, 'is to give our partners value for money by creating new business opportunities for them. For example, we believe HSBC, operating in seventy-six countries around the world, will generate a lot more incremental business than the amount they spend on the Stewart-Ford team.

'To bring more people over to Malaysia is also a priority,' he said, as the corporate talk moved up a gear. 'We regard it as something of a coup to have Texaco on board, as another huge global player with forty thousand outlets. That is,' he stressed, 'forty thousand opportunities for all our sponsors.'

'That's a big commitment for you too,' said Prueller. 'What goal do you have?'

'I never promised anything as a driver and I will say the same as a constructor,' replied Stewart. 'We can only give 100 per cent effort. I would very much like to have a podium finish and a win but to ask that this year is too much. We would like to be in the top ten and pick up championship points. That would be a tremendous achievement.'

When it came to measuring more immediate achievement, the coverage in the newspapers the following morning was an endorsement of the success of the launch and the pulling power of the Stewart name. Almost all of the national daily papers devoted space to the occasion, the broadsheets publishing photographs to give the story added weight and prominence. Compared to subsequent new car media functions – some of which would be a shambles and would deserve the minimal press coverage they received – the launch of the Stewart-Ford SF-1 was a model of professionalism. It was also a good story with a strong human angle. Michael Calvin of the *Daily Telegraph* summed it up best.

He made it sound like it was a one-way street – with Stewart Grand Prix doing the sponsors a favour

'Formula One,' wrote Calvin in the introduction to his piece, 'is an intim-idatingly clinical sport, shaped by corporate ambition, commercial expedience, and technological innovation, but yesterday afternoon it was distilled into flesh and blood.'

Stewart Grand Prix had indeed made a worthwhile impression. Now they had to back that up on the racetrack. The formalities were over for the time being. The team would retreat in private for the next thrilling moment of truth.

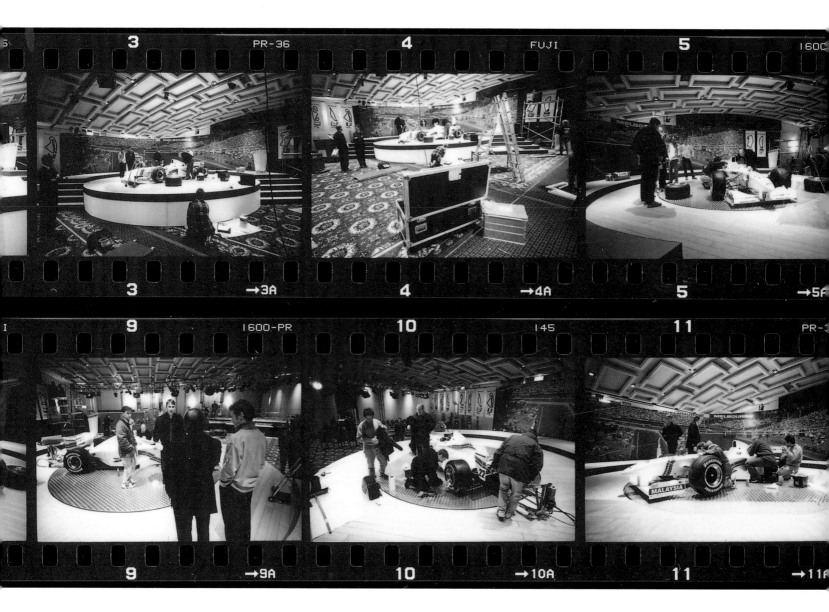

PREVIOUS SPREAD. Launch countdown. Getting the SF-1 ready.

ABOVE. Paul makes himself ready.

RIGHT. A family affair. Paul gives Dylan a reassuring hug during rehearsals.

BELOW. Final preparations in the calm of Jackie's suite.

CHAPTER FIVE

AND THE WHEELS GO ROUND

BOREHAM AIRFIELD, five miles east of Chelmsford, was developed by the American forces in the early 1940s. Appropriately enough, Stewart Grand Prix was returning US investment to this bleak corner of Essex during a dawn raid on 19 December 1996.

It seemed daylight would never break as the plain white transporter edged through the security gate on a cold morning made worse by incessant grey drizzle. There was no pomp or ceremony here. Never had been from the moment the 350-hectare site had been converted from woodland to an aerodrome suitable for the USAAF Martin Marauder bombers. Even when the land reverted to more peaceful purposes and the local car club held motor races on the perimeter track, the events, while occasionally of international status, were scarcely at the forefront of British sport. The final motor race at Boreham was held on 16 December 1952. Forty-four years later, almost to the day, a Grand Prix car would roll onto the tarmac but there was no question of going racing. It would be a cause for celebration if the machine, worth a figure which would have seemed astronomical in 1952, simply ran in a straight line without stopping.

Stewart had chosen Boreham for two reasons. It was reasonably remote. And the Ford Motor Company owned it. The airfield had been bought in 1955 for heavy goods testing and, eight years later, Ford Motorsport moved in to establish one of the most important centres in world rallying. Boreham would be the home of the Ford Escort, the most successful rally car ever built and one which would make a rod for the company's back. Subsequent models – the RS200 and the Sierra Cosworth – would not continue the domination. By December 1996, a revival was underway with the latest Escort Cosworth and, by a quirk of timetabling, the Ford Motorsport department was about to move out of Boreham as the Formula One car rolled in.

The fact that very little had been done over the years to the perimeter road and runways was of little concern to Stewart. All they wanted was peace and privacy and a straight piece of road. Having worked until 3.30 a.m., cosmetic values and deluxe facilities were the last thing on the minds of the engineers and mechanics. They wanted to know whether or not the car worked. No one would have time for the media, and had it been present the intrusive eye of the camera would have created the wrong image as the facilities, if you could call them that, were less than perfect and the team uniforms had not yet been finalized.

They wanted to know whether or not the car worked

The 'shakedown test' is a straightforward trial to ensure that the basics – electrics, electronics, water, and oil systems – work more or less as they should. The severe tests and the fine tuning come at a later stage. For now, it was a case of making sure the engine ran and the wheels turned.

That had seemed an unlikely prospect twenty-four hours before. The shakedown had already been delayed due to problems with the computer software. Normally the software would have been sorted out as the engine ran under more ideal conditions on Cosworth's dynamometer. In this instance, Alan Jenkins and the crew had resorted to sorting the software while running the engine in the workshop – 'it's not something we like to do' – as they attempted to make sure that the car would be ready to run by the 19th.

They chose Boreham's main runway. Base was established at one end, close by the perimeter road with a gravel pit in the background. Otherwise there was nothing to be seen, the horizon lost in the murk. Ford parked a truck alongside Stewart's transporter and a tent covered a rough piece of tarmac measuring approximately thirty feet by thirty feet. An ambulance drew up outside, while inside the coffee flask was the first port of call for mechanics and technicians who had been up all night. The Cosworth engineers, led by Jim Brett, trundled in two banks of monitors which would display information about the Ford-Zetec R engine.

'You may regard a shakedown as not being of much value,' said Brett, 'but it is very important for everyone, Cosworth included. The engine we have installed in the car is the same specification we used in the last race of the season in Japan. We have new developments in hand, of course, but we are using the old specification of engine because it's a known quantity; it gives us a base to work from. The engine may be the same as before, but because this is a new team and a new car, so many things are different about the way things are done and the way the engine has been installed in the car. Everything may look OK on paper and on the test bed but it is not until you actually get the car on the move that you discover whether or not the basics are right.'

Cosworth knew about the value of shakedown tests from hard-won experience. In 1989, they designed a brand new V8 engine. Everything worked perfectly on the bench; the numbers added up on the computers. As soon as the engine went into the Benetton Formula One car, the crankshaft snapped, a disaster as fundamental as a suspension failure the minute the car turns into the first corner. Despite access to sophisticated technical backup, there is no

Inside the coffee flask was the first port of call for mechanics and technicians who had been up all night

substitute for the basic moment of truth which was about to unfold on a cold morning in what seemed like the middle of nowhere.

There were no members of the press on hand, no television crews, no hangers-on. Mark Stewart was recording the moment for posterity. Yet despite the deliberate low-key nature of the occasion there were thirty-two people in the tent, the majority from Ford, Cosworth, Stewart, and trade suppliers such as Bridgestone. And, of course, both drivers.

Since he was still officially employed by Jordan until the end of December, Barrichello looked out of place as he pulled on a brand-new set of plain white overalls, the absence of sponsorship patches ensuring there was no collision of contracts. David Stubbs, the team manager, peeled sponsor logos off the Brazilian's crash helmet while Barrichello realized that his suede driving shoes were not ideal footwear for the wet, uneven tarmac, Jackie Stewart advising him on the benefits of overshoes for an occasion such as this. The mechanics and technicians, meanwhile, were making final preparations to ensure the Stewart-Ford SF-1 got its feet wet for the first time.

A preliminary effort at 9.45 a.m. had the engine burst briefly into life before a problem with the programming brought silence once more. It was another fifty minutes of quiet discussion and much keyboard work at the computer before the engine fired, this time on a more permanent basis. 'Shall we have a look at this?' asked Jenkins as he nodded at the car, his understated rhetorical question signalling that the moment was approaching.

The engine was switched off and final adjustments made as Barrichello climbed into the cockpit. Andy Miller was dispatched to guard the far end of the runway, the tail lights of the Ford Mondeo disappearing into the gloom within a matter of seconds. At 10.51 a.m., the electric blankets were removed from the tyres and the car lowered from the jacks.

'Right?' asks Brett, offering a quick glance at the Stewart personnel gathered round the car. Andy Le Fleming, a former engineer with Ferrari, nods. Brett checks with his technicians at the telemetry screen and then nods to Barrichello and the assembled group. Barrichello raises his hand as a signal to the mechanic crouching with the starter, connected to the rear of the car. The starter whirrs. The engine fires. Barrichello prods the throttle. The revs rise – and keep rising sharply. A mechanic, Alan Maybin, senses trouble. He quickly reaches into the cockpit and flicks off the ignition. There is complete silence for four or five seconds. Then the deep buzz of male voices. It's a problem with the electronically controlled throttle not responding quickly enough. More tapping at the computer keyboard.

It's 11.05 a.m. The engine is started once more. This time the revs respond to Barrichello's actions with his right foot. Everything is fine. The engine cover is replaced and the car is pushed forward a few feet. The tent flaps are opened and Rubens is called forward. Barrichello has a problem finding first gear as he flicks the gear selection control lever, mounted behind the right-hand spoke of the steering wheel.

Clunk! The fresh, sharp metallic sound from the rear of the car indicates he has found the gear. Then the engine stalls. Silence once more. The clutch engagement is very sharp and there is not a lot Barrichello can do about it for the moment. The car is pushed back to allow the starting procedure to take place all over again.

11.08 a.m. The engine fires. The car is pushed forward. First gear is engaged. The engine stalls for a second time. 'OK, Rubens,' says Le Fleming. 'We'll push it right out of the tent next time, then you can give it plenty of revs.' Barrichello, as keen as anyone to get going, nods and looks in his mirror to see if the mechanic with the starter is ready.

11.11 a.m. The engine fires and the car is pushed through the exit. Clunk! This time, the engine revs seriously disturb the air. Barrichello lets out the clutch with his left hand. The rear wheels spin furiously on the wet tarmac. Away she goes! The Stewart-Ford SF-1 is moving under its own power for the first time. It's a runner. At last.

Save for the engineers scrutinizing the telemetry screens, the occupants of the tent decant onto the runway and watch and then listen as the white car is quickly consumed by the damp smog. The gear changes are slow and deliberate, the engine running gently. They can hear Barrichello reach the far end of the runway, about three-quarters of a mile away. Then he accelerates, harder this time, the sound increasing as the dark fuzzy shape emerges, the profile sharpens and becomes white. Even at this stage, the Stewart sounds like a racing car; looks like a racing car. The unspoken thought of everyone present is that they are witnessing a piece of history. Paul Stewart, his coat buttoned to his chin, stands alone and perfectly still, watching intently as Barrichello applies the brakes and points the SF-1 towards the tent. Stewart pauses for a moment, looking for the words. 'A fantastic feeling,' he says simply. It's a moment he won't forget.

The Stewart-Ford SF-1 is moving under its own power for the first time. It's a runner. At last

'The last thing I want to do is to come spinning out of the mist towards you!'

After such an encouraging start, the day did not lose its momentum. Barrichello made two more runs, accelerating with impressive gusto despite an initial limit of 12,000 on the engine revs. By midday the party had been joined by Paul's wife – heavily pregnant with their second son – and Dylan (again, it was difficult to imagine any other Formula One team encouraging such family participation, even assuming they wanted to come in the first place), and Ford's Richard Parry-Jones, Martin Whitaker, and Gwyndaf Evans, winner of the 1996 British Rally Championship in a Ford Escort. The Stewarts were also pleased to see Peter Phillips (and his dog!), the son of the Princess Royal having spent three months gathering work experience at Stewart Grand Prix as he moved through the buying and commercial departments and helped with the launch of the car. This was a far cry from some of the more lavish affairs to which he was accustomed. There was hardly a pause for lunch of sandwiches and chocolate biscuits as the electronics experts worked on raising the engine rev limit and speeding up the gear change, an indication that everyone was keen to get motoring.

Barrichello completed two more runs, the return leg generating much more drama each time as he stayed on the throttle longer and harder, raising enough speed to take sixth gear, the Stewart appearing in a ghostly ball of spray. Barrichello was reaching 170 m.p.h., which was quite fast enough as the stiffly sprung car gave him a rough ride on the elderly runway. When the SF-1 returned to the tent, it brought an aroma of hot oil for the first time. Now it smelt like a racing car.

Barrichello climbed out. 'The bumps are really bad,' he said. 'The last thing I want to do is to come spinning out of the mist towards you! But I tell you, everything is working as it should. I've never been so motivated as this. I must be – to be here in this weather when I could be back in Brazil!'

The enthusiasm was widespread. Jackie Stewart set to work with a cloth, wiping muddy streaks from the bodywork while the technicians pored over the telemetry, devouring the latest information. Everything was shipshape. So far.

At 1.45 p.m. the car emerged once more, Barrichello intent on doing three runs this time. Second gear. Third gear. Then the rhythm was broken. There was a pause before the engine went *blugggghhh* and the car rolled to a halt. Barrichello switched off. The first problem had arrived.

A rescue vehicle, positioned halfway along the runway, and Jackie Stewart's Scorpio (driven by Paul) were the first on the scene. The software had not allowed the gearbox to operate properly but the first priority was to get the car back to the tent. Easier said than done. Paul produced a Moët et Chandon umbrella (a slightly bizarre item to have in this barren hinterland) to give Rubens protection as he remained in the cockpit, his body temperature dropping rapidly. The mechanics, clad in blue sweatshirts, were to experience the same feelings of discomfort after jumping into their Transit van without first donning anoraks. It was bitterly cold as they attempted without success to restart the engine. The car could not be towed because it was stuck in gear. The engine would need to be running in order to at least select neutral. Heavy-duty batteries were called for. But still no success. Forty-five minutes had passed before, as a final resort, it was decided to remove a driveshaft in order to tow the car without wrecking the transmission. With the light fading fast in this remote windswept place, it was decided to call a halt to the day's running.

A few weeks later, the new McLaren would not complete a single lap on its first day out. The latest Ferrari would suffer an engine failure and the Arrows, on which Damon Hill was pinning his hopes for 1997, would belatedly arrive two days late at its shakedown and squeeze in one very slow lap in darkness at Silverstone. By any standards, the baptism of the Stewart-Ford had been a success.

There was a sense of optimism as the mechanics began to pack up and the company dispersed. Jackie Stewart bade his farewells. He was off to join members of the Royal family at Sandringham. On the following Sunday, he would be meeting the Deputy Prime Minister of Malaysia. There would be a positive report to pass on to Dr Mahathir. Everything was in order. So far. Two days before Christmas, in this season of goodwill, the technicians at Stewart Grand Prix would receive a painful kick in the guts.

There was no specific timetable attached to the crash-test programme, the team subjecting the chassis to trials as and when they were ready. On hearing that the test rig at the Cranfield research laboratory would be free on 23 December, Alan Jenkins decided to make use of it for a side-impact trial.

The conditions for the various official tests are clearly defined. Article 15.4.6 of the FIA 1997 Formula One Regulations covers the side-impact test. The key passages stipulate that: '. . . a solid object, having a mass of 780kg and travelling at a velocity of 5 metres per second, will be projected into it (the side of the cockpit area) . . . The resistance of the test structure must be

In this season of goodwill, the technicians at Stewart Grand Prix would receive a painful kick in the guts

such that during the impact the average deceleration of the object does not exceed 10g. All structural damage must be contained within the impact absorbing structure.'

The SF-1 failed that aspect of the test at the first attempt. Or, at least, the first attempt with an FIA representative present. That in itself did not make the test official; the FIA man was merely observing for his own interest, the test itself being part of Stewart's preliminary preparations.

The team had tried using a different material in the construction of part of the chassis. Samples had been checked and repeated tests had proved positive, indicating the material should be capable of withstanding the side impact.

'There was no reason to assume anything else at that stage,' says Jenkins. 'The material had behaved amazingly consistently. It seemed a novel solution. We had done a lot of work with the suppliers and it should have continued to behave the same way, but when we tried it with all the other bits present, a piece of it split off and went further down the chassis than it should have done and it punctured that part of the chassis – which would have been a fail, no argument about that.

'We took a good look at it, saw the problem, and went back to a more conventional form of construction using a sandwich of carbon fibre and aluminium honeycomb. We took that back to Cranfield – and passed the test. End of story. There was another area where we had a small problem with the place where the accident data recorder is housed in the seat back. The regulations – new for 1997 – say it has to go there. We are common with a lot of teams in that the seat back is the major member which stiffens the chassis in the area of the side impact. Now that member has a hole cut in it to accommodate the data recorder. After one of the trial tests, we discovered a small crack. It was absolutely marginal but it would have been a fail so we did something about it.

'The problem we had was that the original fail I referred to was interpreted as some disaster of seemingly global proportions simply because an FIA official was there. It was not a fail, more a part of the experimental process. It had been a last-minute thing on the 23 December. The official was available and, naturally, we thought it would be foolish to pass the test in theory and not have someone there. Anyway, that's when we discovered the problem with the material we were using. We did another test in private and, as I say, when we went for the proper test with the FIA, it passed.

'After one of the trial
tests, we discovered
a small crack'

'The FIA officials are part of the process of getting where you want to be. Charlie Whiting' – the FIA's technical chief – 'has been brilliant over the years. I have had him come to trial tests in the past, for his information as well as mine. It's all part of the learning process, even if it is not interpreted as that sometimes by people outside the team.'

Teams regularly fail at least one section of the impact test during the pre-season trials, but because of the increasingly high profile attached to Stewart their problem attracted a disproportionate amount of attention, which reflected unfairly, in the case of the side impact, on Richard McAinsh, the Senior Chassis Engineer who had gained a fine reputation with composite materials while working for Benetton.

'It was very hard on Richard,' agrees Jenkins. 'I don't think matters were helped when the whole thing was filmed and portrayed as a bit of a disaster. I was never conscious at the time of this tremendous "failure" aspect of the whole thing. It was part of the process, as far as I was concerned. The reason behind all this testing is to make the cars as safe as possible and, in the end, formulate better regulations.

'Having said that, I was a bit disappointed with the way the chassis test had gone. It was a question we had all asked: "Should we do more tests with this material?" We did test it, but not enough. Perhaps we were a bit gung-ho by saying, "Let's put it on the chassis." It kicked us in the guts as a result.'

Nine months before, Jenkins privately admitted that he found it 'scary' to contemplate the thought of having to design and build a new car, and have it running by mid-December. 'On Christmas morning,' mused Jenkins, 'I should be able to sit down, take a deep breath and say, "We did it," because by that time it will have run.'

He was able to relax with his family on 25 December. The car had indeed run, but as Jenkins took time for a glass or two of wine, he knew in his heart of hearts that the hard work had barely started.

ABOVE. Waiting for the off at Boreham. Jackie (centre) with (left to right) Jim Brett, Paul and Rubens.

LEFT. Getting down to detail. Jackie lends a hand with the duster.

ABOVE. Tyre warmers in place, the moment approaches as final preparations are made. RIGHT. Initial impressions from the cockpit. Paul and Egbhal Hamidy listen intently while Jackie gives the bodywork a final wipe.

Making history.
Rubens Barrichello
blasts down the wet
and bumpy straight.

CHAPTER SIX

UPWARDLY MOBILE

T

ON TUESDAY 14 JANUARY 1997, Jackie Stewart hit the floor talking. At 6.30 a.m. he was on the telephone to Malaysia. By 8.00 a.m. he was in the back of his Ford Scorpio. In between conducting taping for this book he was taking calls on his mobile phone, discussing passes for corporate guests at the races which lay ahead, planning a meeting for the following week at the team's headquarters, and organizing a flight to New York, a shooting party at the weekend, and the helicopters for the British Grand Prix. Stewart's home race was not scheduled for another seven months but the popularity of the British round of the championship was such that plans had to be made in advance. Taking to the air was the only way to avoid the chaos in the narrow lanes leading to Silverstone.

Stewart was heading for the Northamptonshire track today. Traffic would not be a problem on this occasion since the team would have the Southern Circuit to themselves (Arrows were supposed to be joining in but delays with their new car meant its shakedown run had been postponed yet again) and members of the public would not be admitted.

Clear air and weak sunshine prevailed as the white tent was erected once more

He was keen to get there. This would be the first run on a proper circuit, as opposed to running up and down the bumpy runway at Boreham one month before. Fast lap times were not expected. Indeed, they would be impossible thanks to the cold weather and a rather silly speed restriction placed on one section of the track. This test, more extensive than the shakedown, would be the final phase of the initial trial before the team headed for Spain and some serious work.

The hope was that the car would simply go out and then come back with nothing untoward happening along the way. On paper, that seemed simple enough but the mechanics and engineers, having worked until 3 a.m. to sort out another problem with the electronics software, knew it might not be as straightforward as that. The only good news late on the Monday night had come from the BBC's weather forecaster: 'After three weeks of freezing conditions,' said Suzanne Charlton, 'there will be no sub-zero temperatures tomorrow. The roads should be free from ice.' And so it proved. Clear air and weak sunshine prevailed as the white tent was erected once more.

The basic layouts of Silverstone and Boreham were almost identical when the aerodromes were built in the forties. They are vastly different now. Silverstone is a centre of motor racing commerce, a place bustling with so much variety that racing almost takes second place. Every square metre is utilized for some form of activity, be it skid control, driver training, off-road instruction, corporate entertainment, exhibitions, conferences, manufacturing (in fifty small industrial units) – and testing, plain and simple.

Stewart had been allocated this northern section of the circuit, the bulk of which used about half of the Grand Prix track itself. The safety facilities attached to the main circuit had been checked by the safety officials representing the FIA, but the link road across the middle, as used by the Southern Circuit, did not have such approval. As a result, the team was subjected to a rule which said Formula One cars could not pass along this section at more than 75 m.p.h. Not that it really mattered to Stewart since out-and-out speed was scarcely the reason behind the exercise, but when a track official – the notorious 'Silverstone Sid' – arrived with a radar gun, the rule was exposed for its absurdity. For a while, it seemed Sid would be fortunate to find a racing car on which to focus his detection device.

This time there were fifty-three people huddled inside the tent. Everyone was involved in some shape or form with a car which was showing little sign of going anywhere. Despite the sunshine the ambient temperature was low enough to require artificial preliminary heating of the engine and gearbox before the machinery could be coaxed into life without causing internal damage.

This amounted to the public debut of the Stewart-Ford. Cameramen moved in to capture the moment

At 11.40 a.m. the first attempt was made to start the engine. Forty minutes later, after further coaxing and computer-driven adjustments, the Ford Zetec-R V10 burst into more permanent song. Rubens Barrichello, now wearing overalls with sponsorship patches, was invited to climb aboard. At 12.38 p.m. the SF-1, equipped with wet-weather tyres, edged through the gap in the crash barrier and ventured onto the empty track. Boreham may have been the first occasion when the car had turned a wheel but this amounted to the public debut of the Stewart-Ford. Cameramen moved in to capture the moment.

As the car became a speck on Hangar Straight, there was not a soul to be seen anywhere round the flat two-mile Southern Circuit. Except, of course, for the group standing motionless by the barrier, collars turned up, eyes scanning the horizon, ears tuned to every rise and fall of the harsh exhaust. You could read their thoughts: 'Is it going to be OK?' There would be nothing more embarrassing than the pregnant silence which would follow an abrupt cessation of engine noise. Particularly on a morning as calm and as still as this.

The V10 kept singing – apart from the brief period as it burbled along the link road in front of the temporary pits in due deference to Sid and his radar gun. Then, once he was back on Hangar Straight, Barrichello floored the throttle with increasing confidence and authority as one lap merged into the next. He completed five in total before returning, as instructed, to the tent. Pressing his thumb on the radio button, Rubens began a nonstop account of his initial impressions: the position of the pedals, the effectiveness of the brakes, the gear ratios, engine response, high engine idle speed, understeer (when the car tries to plough straight on) each time he took his foot off the throttle when entering a corner, the pleasing impression created by the engine when working hard in fifth gear.

The engineers, headsets clamped round their ears, listened, nodded, and made notes. The telemetry gave no nasty warnings of impending doom. Not that the Cosworth engineers had expected any. The engine, which had completed ten miles at Boreham, had since been examined thoroughly, placed on the dynamometer to check its performance, and then returned to Stewart. Apart from a few small problems, which are to be expected on any new installation, nothing untoward had been found. The signs were still good.

Slick tyres were fitted in order to ascertain if the rubber could be made to reach working temperature during the next five-lap run. The sight of Barrichello weaving the car from side to side as he passed the pits, and the sudden urgent crescendos as the tyres, in the extremely cold conditions, struggled for grip on the far side of the circuit, suggested that the plan had not worked. By 1.05 p.m. the car was back in the tent just as the arrival of lasagna and chips in polystyrene trays brought the reminder that it was lunchtime already.

The mechanics and technicians ate on the move as further adjustments were made. Jan Magnussen, having waited quietly on the sidelines all morning, climbed into the back of the truck, and donned a pair of brand-new overalls. Finally his turn had come to drive the car for the first time. Being of small stature, he slipped into the cockpit, and headed onto the track as if he had been driving the car all his life.

The only initial problem he had was with the clutch lever, mounted on the steering wheel. Many drivers prefer this arrangement since it leaves their left foot free to operate the brake pedal, while the right foot builds up engine revs on the throttle at the start of a race – the only time the clutch is used, except

The telemetry gave no nasty warnings of impending doom

when leaving the pits. Magnussen had difficulty operating the lever as he moved off from a standstill while turning the steering wheel at the same time. It was something he would become accustomed to. Apart from that, his only problem was incorrect adjustment of the six-point seat harness.

After another handful of laps it was clear that the Dane was bored with the limitations imposed by the rain tyres and the speed limit. The tedium was interrupted by an unexpected visit to the pits forced by the disappearance of the dashboard lights, an important part of the monitoring system. The problem had been caused by a poor connection following the earlier removal of the steering wheel to check the clutch.

A lengthier stay in the pits occurred five laps later when Magnussen requested an adjustment to the brakes. By the time he had returned to the track at 3.54 p.m. the beginning of a perfect sunset meant the track had begun to freeze at Club Corner. Nature had called a reasonably successful test to a close.

As always, the team was hungry to learn more. Even so, it was admitted that the day had served its purpose. They knew that the car started, stopped, changed gear, and negotiated corners. But very little else. Running at speed would have exposed any weaknesses in the machinery. That would have to wait until the first proper test during a demanding few days in Spain.

In the meantime, Jackie Stewart had work to do. Mokhzani Mahathir, the son of the Malaysian Prime Minister, had come to take a look at his country's investment. Having shown him around the car, Jackie made sure the photographers caught the influential guest on camera as he posed with the two drivers. Then it was time for a final chat with Barrichello and Magnussen, Jackie telling the Dane that he would be the centre of attention during the forthcoming weeks. Neither driver needed reminding. Stewart had already arranged for them to visit the tailor he had used for the previous twenty-five years. He had organized handmade shoes and taken care of other aspects of presentation by booking them into a consultant who would advise on the art of public speaking. Nothing was left to chance, no detail remained unchecked. That had been Stewart's creed ever since he started racing and nothing was going to change him now.

On the way home, he returned calls to journalists from a newspaper in Australia and a holiday magazine; they had phoned his office earlier in the day in search of interviews. Each writer was treated with courtesy, the thoughtful and articulate replies giving the impression that this was the first time the

By the time he had returned the track had begun to freeze

particular questions had been asked even though they had been dealt with many times before.

What next? The trip to New York; a few details needed taking care of. Stewart dialled a British Airways number dedicated to VIPs. Referring to the Concorde flight the next day, he confirmed his reservation of seat 1A, surely the most prestigious allocation in world travel. Then he asked the reception-ist to advise JFK Airport that a film crew would be waiting to film his arrival. Rather than demanding, Jackie made his point tactfully. 'I really don't expect you to stop everything and change the world,' he explained in his usual cheer-ful manner, 'but any help you can give would be appreciated. Thanks very much . . . oh, and by the way, I'll be flying back with you on Friday.'

It was 5.30 p.m. on Tuesday as the Ford Scorpio, driven by Gerry Webb, Jackie's chauffeur for eighteen years, crossed the M4 motorway and aimed for Sunningdale. With time running short a plan to visit the gymnasium was shelved, and Stewart headed for a modern penthouse apartment which was not 'home' in the strictest sense. It was a mark of his dedication to the new team that in order to be close to the headquarters in Milton Keynes he had decided to abandon the shores of Lake Geneva and the beautiful property his family had called home since 1968. Clayton House had everything: pool, sauna, tennis courts, a magnificent location. It had taken twenty-eight years to create.

In order to be close to the headquarters in Milton Keynes he had decided to abandon the shores of Lake Geneva

The move was a terrible wrench, not least because Boss and Bugsy, a Norfolk terrier and a black Labrador, had been placed in quarantine. Twice-weekly visits to the kennels in Bracknell were just about the only moments of relaxation Jackie and Helen had been able to enjoy in the difficult and faintly traumatic aftermath of the move from Switzerland. The dogs were well cared for, but having been accustomed to the freedom of six acres a compound measuring twelve square yards was a shock to all concerned. Worse still, there was no view. Jackie and Helen arranged to have a small staircase built to allow the pets to see the outside world. The fact that the steps had been carpeted should be no surprise.

On 14 January there was less than a month to endure before the pets' release, just about the only positive side of a calendar which seemed jet-propelled as the first race rushed to meet the Stewarts and their team. The Australian Grand Prix was only six weeks away; everything would need to be packed and ready in five. Three cars would be required and yet they had barely started running with the first. That would begin six days later in Spain.

Formula One teams choose to travel to southern Europe in pursuit of reasonable weather during the winter months. It was ironic therefore to find the Jerez track doused with rain during the first day of serious running with the Stewart-Ford SF-1. Magnussen went first, completing twenty-six laps in roughly ten-minute bursts before returning to the pits each time for adjustments and, more important, to have the car checked for any signs of imminent failure. Barrichello was given a turn in the gathering gloom at the end of the day in preparation for a longer run the following morning.

In the event, a gearbox oil leak would confine his activity to twenty laps. But that was enough to confirm Barrichello's initial suspicion that the car was basically without serious vices. Despite the comparatively raw state of a new car, it will either be competitive from the word go – or not. The fine tuning will make a good car better. But it will not make a bad car good. Barrichello was in no doubt about SF-1. 'I tell you,' he beamed, 'this car is good!' It was said as much in relief as in excited anticipation. The drivers took turns to complete another forty-one laps on the final day, Barrichello constantly in and out of the pits as changes to the set-up were evaluated. So far, so good.

In the late afternoon, Magnussen was coming to the end of his stint when the car was pitched into a spin as he came through the corner leading onto the pit straight. It was not the sort of place where you would expect a driver to make an error. In any case, he had not been trying particularly hard. The engineers feared the worst as they checked the car. A link on the rear suspension was found to have failed.

'It was a toe-link,' recalls Jenkins. 'All the combined cases had not been taken into account when calculating the forces involved. In tension and compression, the part had more than enough reserve, but even though the buckling reserve on the toe-link was more than sufficient, under load it had deflected slightly. We were in the process of setting up a rig to do all the deflection tests which were not so much safety-critical but as a means of determining whether the suspension geometry was being maintained properly in terms of the stability and handling. Because we had been unable to check it fully, we hadn't realized it was deflecting slightly which, in turn, put a little bit of bending in the toe-link itself.

'It was down to me. I had a range of people working on the project and it is a matter of how far I could let them go without looking at every single thing. You learn how to do it as you get to know people better. As I go through

Magnussen was coming to the end of his stint when the car was pitched into a spin

each case and sign it off, I have to make a judgement and decide whether or not it has been done properly. In that case, one aspect had not been taken fully into account. The loadings, as laid down in the book, had looked correct. But if you had applied bending at the same time, then they wouldn't have been correct. It was a design issue in terms of the calculations involved. It was not done as well as it should have been.'

At least there was time to carry out modifications before the next test, scheduled for Barcelona a fortnight later. The Jerez test had brought the team into the public domain, Paul Stewart admitting that his pulse had quickened when he saw the Ferrari transporter parked in the paddock. This was serious. Small wonder there was a surge of excitement when Barrichello proved to be faster than Michael Schumacher when the Stewart and the Ferrari were out together on a wet track. The Jerez test had been reasonable, but as yet there had been no serious and consistent running. That would be taken care of on the Circuit de Catalunya.

The weather played its part, perfect conditions – clear skies, sunshine, and a cool breeze – encouraging the desire to get out there and give the car some stick. The drivers wanted to extend themselves as well, the Barcelona track in the dusty foothills to the north-west of the city being fast and demanding. Barrichello described it as a good 'physical' track, one which would test his neck muscles and generally tone up his body in a way which no amount of work in a gymnasium could manage.

The tempo had increased noticeably thanks to the presence of Arrows and Ligier and the sound of cars blasting past the pits, engines singing their hearts out on the long straight. A few days before, Jacques Villeneuve had laid down a substantial marker by shattering the unofficial lap record with a time of 1m 18.8s in the brand-new Williams-Renault.

There was still only one Stewart-Ford available and Barrichello had it once the car had been made ready to run on the first day. He completed a number of laps but further time was lost while the gear ratios were changed, a job which would become a matter of routine but on this occasion took longer than usual because it was the first time the mechanics had done it at a racetrack. It was another part of the vast learning process.

There were no more than fifteen personnel present, a relief from the cast of thousands which had attended the initial running at Silverstone. The conditions were more workmanlike in every sense. The tent had made way for a

There was a surge of excitement when Barrichello proved to be faster than Michael Schumacher

spacious well-lit garage, giving the team the chance to practice setting up the backdrop of banners carrying logos and sponsor identification. A gantry had been made ready, which would be positioned over the car and carry additional lighting and a location for the power lines and connections to the telemetry, these cables dropping neatly down to the car rather than snaking untidily across the garage floor. The Stewart-Ford team at least looked the part.

Mind you, these were still early days and improvisation remained the watch word. The gantry had been equipped with red and green lights, a simple but effective way of allowing the Ford and Cosworth technicians, glued to their telemetry screens arranged behind the partition, to signal that they had finished downloading and the mechanics were free to disconnect the data-acquisition cable from the car. The red light was working but the lens for the green light had not been made ready in time. The problem was quickly solved by judicious use of scissors and the end of a plastic bottle of Highland Spring water.

While the ratios were being changed, the fortunes of Stewart's rivals were varying dramatically. Damon Hill's Arrows was towed back to the pit lane after breaking down yet again. Not long before that, Olivier Panis had shattered Villeneuve's time with a lap of 1m 18.3s. Food for thought as the Stewart team considered Barrichello's laps in the 1m 20s mark, with the occasional dip into 1m 19s. But these were early days.

The mechanics worked until midnight. 'We could have stopped earlier,' said David Stubbs. 'But you know how it is with a new car – we were just fiddling about towards the end, having a good look at everything, seeing what we could improve. Anyway,' he smiled, 'it wasn't too bad. The bar was still open when we got back to the hotel. And at least we were better off than the guys next door.'

He was referring to the Arrows and Yamaha technicians. Having replaced a broken engine that evening, they had fired up the new one at midnight, just to check that everything was working properly in readiness for the morning. Incredibly, within a couple of minutes, the fresh engine had failed as well. The weary mechanics had no option but to roll out another Yamaha V10 and start all over again.

Breakfast was served by Stewart's catering staff in the garage next door at 7 a.m., the mechanics having already scraped the ice off the minibus windscreen as the dramatic temperature variation made itself felt. The circuit was opened at 9 a.m. It was a waste of time. Fog had descended, adding to the

Damon Hill's Arrows was towed back to the pit lane after breaking down yet again

chill and ruling out track activity since one marshals' post could not see the next. Gradually, long shadows appeared in the pit lane as the hazy sun made its gradual climb from behind the grandstand opposite. By 10.45 a.m. Barrichello was dressed for action and preparing to join Panis and Hill as they ventured onto the circuit.

The morning was spent in and out of the pits as various adjustments to the springs and ride heights were tried. Ligier, meanwhile, were making a nonstop run, something of a luxury which indicated how far the French team had got with their preparations. Hill, meanwhile, had trailed into the pits with yet another engine failure. He climbed silently from his car and glared at the back of the Arrows. If looks could kill . . .

Despite the regular visits to the pits, Barrichello and Andy Le Fleming were very pleased with the morning's work. 'The car is doing everything it should when we make the changes,' said the engineer. 'Yes,' Barrichello agreed. 'The changes are working out exactly as I would have hoped. But the thing is, it really feels nice. I'm really enjoying driving it!'

He had one final run before stopping and handing over to Magnussen at 2 p.m. Jan was raring to go; he had only driven the car for a total of nine laps in dry weather, and as the temperature reached 62° he wanted to make the most of the continuing perfect conditions. As the mechanics began the process of swapping the drivers' seats, the sound of engines on the track was replaced by the patter of feet as photographers and officials sprinted up the pit lane.

Panis had crashed heavily at the exit of the last corner, a very quick right-hander – fortunately with a sizeable run-off area. The rear suspension had broken and the Frenchman had been a passenger as the car was hurled across the gravel trap and into a tyre barrier lining a concrete wall. Panis was unhurt. The damaged car was unceremoniously returned to the Ligier garage on the back of a breakdown lorry. By the time Magnussen was settling into his first run, the Ligier transporter was already leaving the paddock and heading towards the team's headquarters in Magny-Cours. Their visit had been prematurely curtailed and there was some serious thinking to be done. Better to discover such problems now rather than later. That, after all, was the purpose of the test session.

Magnussen immediately ran into trouble with overheating brakes, the Dane being harsher in his braking technique than Barrichello. There was nothing wrong with that; the team now knew they would need to cater for it by fitting

Panis had crashed heavily at the exit of the last corner

larger cooling ducts, although it was later discovered that, by using a left-foot braking technique, Magnussen had been riding the pedal unnecessarily. The following day, Sunday, he got down to the longest uninterrupted run so far for both the car and the driver when he completed twenty-two laps. At no stage did he have a low load of fuel or fresh tyres. His lap times in the low 1m 22s reflected that but Magnussen was more interested in learning about the car than creating headlines. He had completed a total of thirty-five laps by the time he handed the car back to his team-mate for the final twenty laps of the three-day programme.

On his twelfth lap of the afternoon Barrichello recorded a time of 1m 18.9s, just half a second away from the best lap established by Panis and a full 1.7 seconds inside the pole-position time for the 1996 Spanish Grand Prix. It was a fair indication of the potential of the SF-1. Rivals sat up and took notice for the first time. This was exactly what the team needed as they packed up and prepared to move south to Estoril in Portugal.

'It's been really satisfying to get some laps under my belt,' enthused Magnussen. 'I can now go to Estoril, get back into the rhythm quickly, and hopefully do some more long runs.'

If only Grand Prix racing was that simple.

OPPOSITE, TOP. Another day, another step forward. The sun rises above the grandstand on the Circuit de Catalunya.

OPPOSITE, BOTTOM. The romance of it all. Fog hinders early running at Barcelona.

ABOVE. Looking and listening. Engineers Andy Le Fleming (left), Jean-François
Sinteff and Rob Preston (right) monitor Barrichello as he blasts into sight on
the main straight at Barcelona.

Not a soul in sight.
The lonely business
of testing.

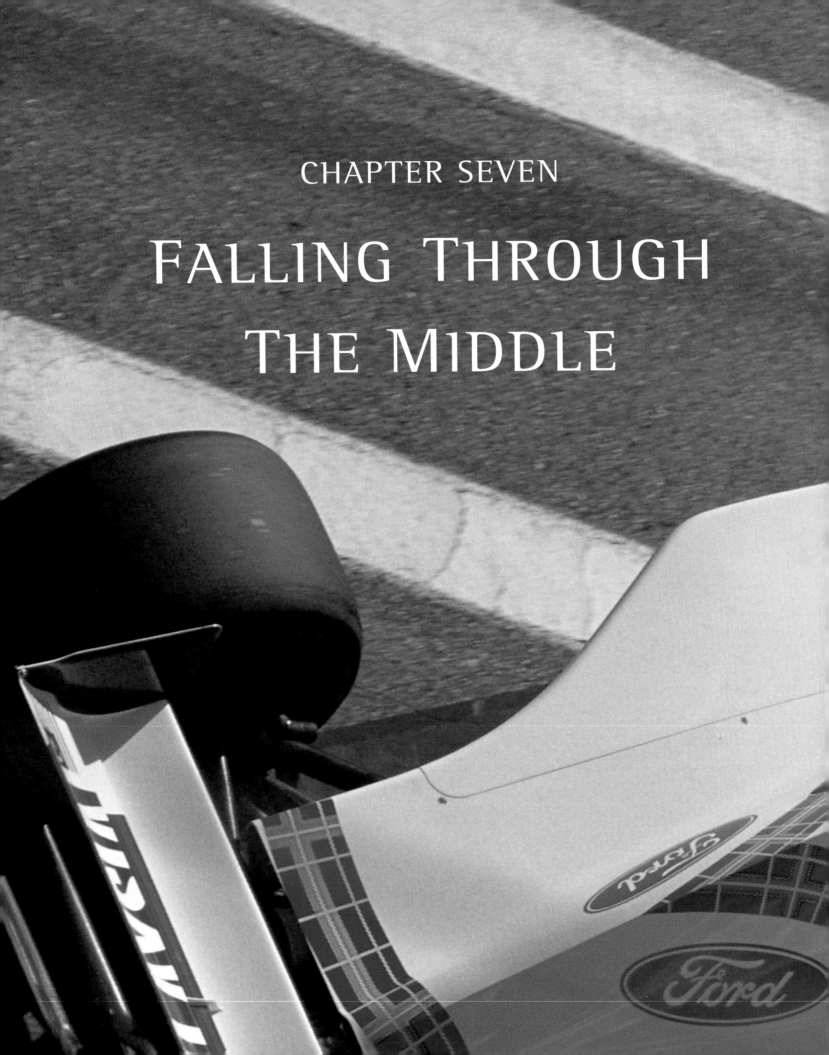

CHAPTER SEVEN

FALLING THROUGH THE MIDDLE

ESTORIL BOASTED one of the most demanding corners in motor racing, a two-part affair at the end of the 180 m.p.h. main straight. The track flicked right, swept downhill briefly, and then funnelled into another very fast right-hander before continuing to plunge towards a hairpin. It was a sequence which sorted the men from the boys. If your car was handling well, the thrill of driver and machine working in harmony at such a pace had no equal. If your car was proving difficult, the first corner at Estoril provided a fierce test of reactions, commitment, and bravery.

The fact was, if you were going to have an accident in the second part of the corner then it was going to hurt, simply because there was nowhere to go. A natural valley beyond the rock face on the outside of the corner meant it was impossible to provide a run-off area. As a result the crash barrier ran along the edge of the track, a three-tier wall of steel towering above the cars as they sweep past, less than a foot away, at 150 m.p.h. It paid not to even think about the consequences of something going wrong.

When the Stewart-Ford went into the barrier, it hit very hard

Jan Magnussen had left the pits, running a set of brand-new tyres for the first time ever on the Stewart-Ford. Not knowing what to expect from the fresh rubber, he had taken it easy on his first lap. Now he was starting to push. Going through the first part of the right-hander, he felt the rear of the car slide more than usual. His first thought was that perhaps the grip from the tyres was not as good as he had anticipated. He pressed on. A firm flick of the wheel committed him to the second part of the corner. When the rear of the car felt very loose, much worse than before, he knew he could be in trouble. Here, of all places.

Magnussen corrected the first slide. The car straightened, but as he tried to get back on course and sweep through the rest of the corner the back of the car lurched out of line. This time, there was no chance of recovery.

The SF-1 had spun quickly through 180° by the time it had reached the outside of the corner, where the shiny bevelled edge of the kerb appeared to suck the car upwards and towards the waiting metal. When the Stewart-Ford went into the barrier, it hit very hard, the right front wheel taking the brunt of the impact.

Magnussen felt the calf of his left leg being pinched by metal as part of the right front suspension punched its way through the chassis wall and straight across the width of the cockpit. He did not feel any pain as such. His initial reaction, that the injury might be limited to bruising, was followed instantly by the fear that the car might swipe the barrier again and cause real pain. A broken leg was the last thing he wanted at such a vital stage in his career.

The car jerked backwards off the kerb and came to a halt without further contact. Magnussen tried to climb out but found his left leg was trapped. A couple of marshals and a doctor soon appeared on the scene. The medical officer quickly ascertained that the driver was perfectly OK but the marshals could not work out precisely what was holding him in the cockpit. When Andy Le Fleming and Dave Redding arrived, they found the marshals preparing tools capable of cutting through the chassis.

The officials' concern for Magnussen's speedy exit was commendable but such drastic measures filled the engineer and chief mechanic with horror. If let loose with such powerful equipment, the marshals could write off the chassis in a matter of minutes. It was not what anyone at Stewart Grand Prix needed at this juncture.

Redding peered into the chassis tub. He could see that the suspension arm had gone through the loose material of Magnussen's driving suit, the bit which had been hanging beneath his calf muscle on his outstretched left leg. After Redding had used a penknife to laboriously cut through the triple layers of flame-proof material in such a confined space, Magnussen was eventually freed. With the left leg of his driving suit in tatters, he climbed from the cockpit and walked to the waiting ambulance.

'It was a big shock for me,' admitted Paul Stewart. 'I actually heard the bang from the pits. It was a sickening sound and we knew it had to be Jan. When I got to the scene, I was surprised to find other drivers – Gerhard Berger, Jean Alesi, and Heinz-Harald Frentzen – there as well, seeing what they could do for Jan. It really brought home to me how quickly things can change in Formula One. You're up one minute and down the next. You can go from good to bad in seconds. It graphically emphasized the responsibility involved and the consequences of what I had taken on.'

The local hospital confirmed that Magnussen's injuries had been confined to a small cut requiring six stitches on his leg. Jan could consider himself very fortunate. The damage to the car would have a more paralysing effect on the team's elaborate plans.

Stewart Grand Prix had booked into Estoril for four days. This would be the first opportunity to run both cars together, an important stage in the learn-

'It was a sickening sound and we knew it had to be Jan'

ing curve. Until now, there had only been one car in use during each test session. That meant just one radio frequency in operation, one set of telemetry, one plan of attack, one group of mechanics. Having two cars would allow David Stubbs to iron out the wrinkles which were bound to occur as the team reached full steam for the first time and lines of communication became crossed. The second chassis had been completed overnight and flown to Lisbon on the day Magnussen had his crash, the shipment having cost £10,000, which was not to be taken lightly given that the budget was tight. Now the team was in a quandary. What exactly had happened to Magnussen's car? Would it be safe to run the second chassis once the final touches had been added in the garage?

It was quickly discovered that the left rear suspension had broken. It was a failure which drove a stake through the collective hearts of the team management. Whereas the suspension problem in Jerez had been from a design error, one of those miscalculations which can occur, this was due to a sequence of events which, in a perfect world, should not have been allowed to happen.

In the hectic environment surrounding the formation of a team and the running of a new car, perfection is a luxury. But what really annoyed Alan Jenkins was the fact that this could have been avoided, indeed should have been avoided in view of the fact that they were about to run at Estoril and commit their car and drivers to the demands of the treacherous first corner.

Jenkins had underscored the entire test programme with the essential proviso that components, particularly those under stress, should be checked at regular intervals, even if this meant disrupting a long-distance test. In other words, even though the team desperately needed to see how the car stood up to a sixty-lap run, he would insist that the car stop every twenty laps in order to permit an inspection. And if the check gave the slightest cause for concern, then the test would be delayed so that the part in question could be removed and subjected to a more rigorous examination.

Either way, plans had been laid to crack-test everything on the car between Barcelona and the test a few days later at Estoril. Unfortunately, this coincided with a change of crew as the mechanics on duty in Spain flew home in order to give another group experience of working on the car in Portugal. Due to a communications problem typical of the type to be expected in any new organization, the suspension parts were not checked as thoroughly as they should have been. A fault in the welding procedure on the left rear wishbone was not

What really annoyed Alan Jenkins was the fact that this could have been avoided

detected and the part in question was put back on the car. The tiny crack and, more important, the weakness in the team's procedures, was about to be graphically exposed.

'There were no excuses,' says Jenkins. 'But it did show that it is harder than you would think to introduce procedures from scratch. In a team that has been running for many years, the procedures have been established over a long period of time. What happens is, these teams do not test the bits that are actually running on the car. The parts are simply taken out of service, removed for checking, and, in the meantime, replaced with new ones so that the running of the car can continue. The checks are carried out in the relative comfort of the factory situation. If the parts have been removed after, say, two hundred kilometres, then they will have been checked by the time the replacement parts have reached that figure.

'Once you have been through the pre-season testing and passed the first race, everything levels out. But with a new car you worry about the build-up until you have got a few thousand kilometres on everything. This was a genuine new-team thing. The intention was there, but with the changeover of crews, the one crucial bit fell through the middle. And at Estoril of all places.

'It so happened that a Danish film crew had been standing on the inside of the corner when Jan went off. They let us have a copy of the video. I sat and watched it two or three times. I am completely obsessed with trying to avoid things like that happening, trying to avoid hurting anyone. It was horrible to watch. Very painful.'

In the meantime, the work had to go on. A modification would be necessary and that, of course, would affect the second car. It was possible to have the revised suspension components made in the factory and shipped to Portugal. Since the test could be extended by at least one day without interfering too much with the final preparations for the first Grand Prix, the team could run both cars for a limited period. That was the logical answer.

Unfortunately, Spanish truck drivers had chosen to go on strike and effectively jam the route home. Stubbs could not risk having his transporter stuck in Spain. There was less than three weeks before the cars and equipment were due to be presented at Stansted Airport for shipment to Melbourne. The risk was too great. It was decided to give the second chassis a brief shakedown run and then pack up. It was a serious blow to the programme.

The final irony would come when, after continual concern over the two

'I am completely obsessed with trying to avoid things like that happening . . . it was horrible to watch'

corners at Estoril and perhaps prompted by Magnussen's accident, the sport's governing body decided to take action. Changes were requested which, while altering the challenging character of the corners in question, would nevertheless reduce the element of risk in the event of a mechanical failure. The Portuguese authorities dithered over the implementation of the alterations to such an extent that the Grand Prix was struck from the 1997 calendar. So Stewart would not be racing at Estoril in any case.

The truck made good progress across southern Spain and passed through the Spanish–French border without any unnecessary delay. Now Stubbs had to take stock. With time running out, the best they could do was fall back on Silverstone on Monday 24 February and hope for a decent break in the weather. In the event, it was the gearbox hydraulics which failed to cooperate, leaving the team to resort to one final run at the Northamptonshire track the following Wednesday.

The storms of the previous couple of days had subsided to blustery and bitterly cold conditions. Stewart were not alone, Benetton, Tyrrell, McLaren, Jordan, and Lola also using Silverstone for final preparations. One quick look in each garage would indicate the state of readiness of the team in question.

At McLaren and Benetton – serious rivals to Williams, the championship favourites – the mood was relaxed and routine. The cars were ready and the purpose of the day was to carry out a final check, the equivalent of a post-service road test by your local garage. At McLaren, all three cars (one each for David Coulthard and Mika Hakkinen, plus a spare car) were squatting in the vast garage, only a skeleton staff of mechanics on hand as the drivers completed a handful of laps each before going home.

In the Stewart garage there was just one car. And it was, as usual, the focus of feverish attention. Far from being a final shakedown, this was a continuation of the climb up a learning curve which now seemed near vertical. Barrichello having returned to Brazil to get married, the driving was being done by Magnussen. Apart from everything else, the Dane was worried about his leg, the stitches from the Estoril injury having burst open the previous evening. It would not hinder his progress on the track, which was more than could be said for the car.

After a few laps, a rubber boot on one of the drive shafts split open and deposited lubricant where it wasn't wanted. It was a failure which happens from time to time. The feeling was, why did it have to happen now? It was

This was a continuation of the climb up a learning curve which now seemed near vertical

difficult not to think that the start of the season had arrived far too quickly. There was much to be done and no longer any time to do it. The team still had not run two cars together. There had not been any chance to practice a pit stop, the crucial refuelling rehearsal having been limited to a run with a car on the factory floor, a far cry from the urgency of a hot and noisy machine screaming to a halt in the pit lane. Magnussen at least was able to practise coming to a precise stop at predetermined points in the pit lane; he also took the opportunity to pull up on the pit straight and make a full-blooded racing start for the first time. Tick those two items from a long list.

As the team packed up at the end of the day, one of the few comforts was the truism that there is always someone worse off than yourself. Damon Hill and Arrows, running miles behind schedule, had turned up in the afternoon, Hill completing just one lap before the nose wing fell off. It was difficult to think of a more fundamental and humiliating failure. At least Stewart Grand Prix had not suffered any such embarrassment, the team's difficulties being limited to seemingly endless teething problems, of which more lay in store at the factory that night.

Magnussen had been driving chassis number two, the car which had been flown to Estoril but had only received a limited amount of running. Once back at the factory, the car would be stripped down, checked over, and the components crack-tested before being rebuilt as far as possible prior to being made ready for shipment to Stansted the following morning. Meanwhile, the third car was being completed at the factory. The first time it would turn a wheel would be when official practice began in Melbourne, a less than ideal situation but one which was unavoidable thanks to the accident in Estoril.

The chassis which Magnussen had crashed – number one – had been repaired and would act as the spare car in Australia. However, with the production facilities being stretched to the limit just to service the two race cars, a shortage of parts meant that the spare car would be completed in Australia, as and when the bits became available. While all of this was going on at the factory, the truck crews were packing the mountain of parts and spares into purpose-made boxes. Or, at least, they should have been.

The box manufacturer had taken on too much, and while some of the containers had been delivered the residue of the order would not arrive until five o'clock the following morning, three hours before everything was supposed to be ready for movement to the airport. Stubbs had no alternative but to call

A shortage of parts meant that the spare car would be completed in Australia

the freight agent at Stansted, explain his predicament, and plead for more time. The loading schedule for the Boeing 747 freighters carrying the British teams' cars and equipment was altered to accommodate him. That was one piece of good news at the end of yet another long night in Milton Keynes.

There was little romance attached to the thought that they were finally heading for the glamour of their first Grand Prix in sunny Australia. It was simply another deadline which had been stretched to the limit. But they had made it. Finally, they were going racing. After a frantic few months, it was good to be getting down to business, even if the prospect caused an understandable degree of apprehension.

David Stubbs, Dave Redding, and the truck crews flew out of London on Friday 28 February, exactly one week before practice was due to start in Melbourne. Not having been to the circuit before, Stubbs wanted to check out the garage they had been allocated and begin planning the layout. Before the cars and the mechanics arrived he needed to oversee the erection of rooms at the back of the garage for the team's technical management, the engineers from Ford, the public relations department, and the catering staff. An area would have to be set aside to accommodate guests as they had lunch and watched the television pictures. Meanwhile, at the front of the garage, the background banners would need to be erected around the bay in which the three cars would be worked on under the gaze of rivals, the media, and passers by in the pit lane. Ready or not, Stewart Grand Prix was about to go on public display.

The mechanics duly arrived on Monday to find that Stubbs and the advance party had sorted out the boxes and the cars in readiness. Meanwhile, back at the factory, production continued, Alan Jenkins being one of the last to leave England with suitcases which carried more than his toothbrush and a change of clothes.

It is a common sight at the beginning of any Grand Prix season to have boxes and packages of odd shapes and sizes tumble onto the baggage carousel at the first port of call. Last-minute changes and preparations affect every team, big and small. Jenkins was musing on that very thought as he waited for an extremely heavy suitcase to appear at Melbourne airport. Inside were small but vital bits necessary for the completion of each car.

The black and slightly grubby Samsonite never appeared. Jenkins, although frustrated, was scarcely surprised. He had been working in motor racing far

After a frantic few months, it was good to be getting down to business

too long not to know that nothing ever runs true to form. The next problem was to discover precisely where the missing piece had gone, a task which was complicated straightaway by the news – unknown to anyone in Australia – that the case had never been loaded onto the aircraft in the first place. By the time the Samsonite had been found in London, the start of the Grand Prix season was about to burst noisily into life on the far side of the world.

ABOVE. Taking shape. The garage partitions now in place, Paul, Jackie and Alan Jenkins discuss the latest developments.
OPPOSITE. Magnussen finally begins some serious running.

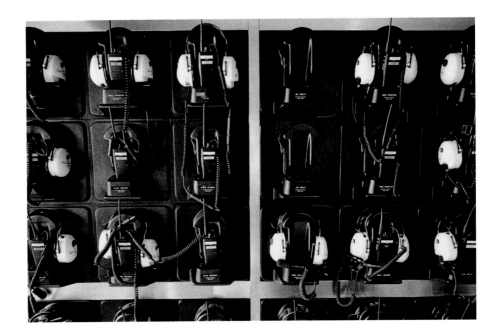

ABOVE. All ears. Headsets, vital for communication when engines are running, recharge on the racks in the garage.

OPPOSITE. Now what? Magnussen's pensive look becomes all too familiar.

CHAPTER EIGHT

TOO LATE
NOW

THE MORNING NEWSPAPERS on Friday 7 March carried extensive previews of the Australian Grand Prix. It was inevitable that comparisons should be made with the first day of term because the Melbourne paddock was exactly like an upmarket school quadrangle where old acquaintances were resumed and gossip updated. Ahead lay months of hard work but meanwhile there was time to enjoy the build-up of anticipation which is unique to the opening encounter of any international sporting series.

Speculation was rampant. Could Jacques Villeneuve and Williams live up to their roles as pre-season favourites? How would Heinz-Harald Frentzen fare as Hill's replacement? Did Damon know something we didn't about the potential of his new team, Arrows-Yamaha? Would the Ferrari be more reliable than before? What contribution, if any, would Bridgestone make? And how would the new boys fare? The newspapers and magazines examined every angle and it was not surprising to find profiles of Stewart, father and son, featuring across a broad spectrum of publications.

Paul knew he had finally arrived in the big time on the Thursday when an official press conference, called by the governing body, the FIA, had him sharing the platform in the circuit media room with Damon Hill and Michael Schumacher. Paul spoke with enthusiasm about the team's efforts. He explained how the learning curve had been steep and would continue to climb. The goal would be to score a few points by the end of the season. Stewart Grand Prix were under no illusions but, like everyone else in Melbourne, they couldn't wait to get started. Finally they would discover just where they stood in comparison with the eleven other teams preparing in the pit lane below.

In some respects, Melbourne was the perfect place to launch a new season. The city provided a wide choice of hotels and facilities to cater for every need. It would have been a different story, for instance, if the first race had been held among more down-at-heel surroundings in São Paulo. Melbourne, anxious to counter the chest-beating of Sydney and its capture of the Olympics in 2000, wanted to demonstrate a capacity to host an international event. For Stewart Grand Prix, however, this was perhaps the worst place for their debut, since Melbourne could not have been further from home. The logistics and costs involved, not to mention the worry of having brought everything they might need, was a major hurdle before a car even ventured onto the track.

> This was perhaps the worst place for their debut, since Melbourne could not have been further from home

The Albert Park circuit, although man-made and running inside suburban parkland, was a fine example of planning and endeavour. The track layout was reasonably demanding and the organization second to none. Nothing was too much trouble, so much so that Grand Prix racing seemed to be made for Melbourne. And, equally, Stewart Grand Prix seemed to be made for Formula One.

That was evident from the frequent visitors to the front of the team's garage. Formula One has a clear and immovable pecking order determined by the accumulation of championship points the previous year. The reigning Constructors' Champions, Williams, occupied the garages at the head of the pit lane, the rest taking up position according to their standing in the points table. Stewart and Lola, newcomers in 1997, were squeezed in at the far end.

It was a fair stretch from Williams to Stewart. The crowds outside the garage doors would thin out the further they were removed from Williams and Ferrari. And yet there was always a pocket of photographers, journalists and rival team-members peering in through the doors at Stewart-Ford. Frank Williams had his wheelchair pushed the length of the pit lane specifically to wish the Stewarts luck. Ron Dennis, the boss of McLaren, also made the trip. Other team managers did the same.

These generous gestures did nothing to dispel the plain fact that when push came to shove the Stewarts would be on their own in a deeply competitive environment. Equally, the team drew satisfaction from the reaction as rival mechanics and engineers stood their distance and cast critical eyes over the garage. The more seasoned members of Stewart-Ford had seen it all before. They had done the same thing themselves when working for established teams in the past. Nothing needed to be said but they could read the expressions. The body language said their critical audience was suitably impressed. The team looked as if it had been around for years. Now Stewart-Ford had to take the next step and talk with confidence on the racetrack.

As the time approached for practice to begin at 11 a.m. on Friday, engines were warmed up in readiness and then switched off. The mechanics made final checks, the gleaming bodywork received one more polish. Paul and Jackie walked through the garage, cameras clicking from the door as photographers focused on the Racing Stewart tartan trousers worn by father and son. Team-members, having been expecting to see such startling attire, grinned when they saw the reactions of bystanders.

The body language said their critical audience was suitably impressed

Very little was said because, in truth, minds were on other things. Andy Le Fleming, his headset already in place, murmured quietly that he felt very nervous. The waiting as the final minutes ticked by was not helping anyone. Finally, Rubens Barrichello picked up his helmet and flameproof balaclava. 'OK,' he said to no one in particular, 'let's go to work.'

At last. After all these months of talking and planning and testing, there would be serious action. Or, at least, there would be for some.

On a day when each driver usually completes thirty laps, the maximum allowed, Barrichello would manage a total of six. He had barely got going. His taut expression said as much as he removed his helmet for the last time that day. The timing screen showed that the Brazilian was twenty-first fastest of the twenty-four entries. He had managed just one timed lap.

Magnussen, having run off the track briefly at one stage, was eighteenth fastest. He, too, had not been without his problems. The cars had spent more time in the garage than they had on the circuit. This was to be expected on the very first day. Even so, it was frustrating for a team which knew it could compete and wanted to show its worth.

The day had its lighter moment as George Harrison called in. The former Beatle is a fan of Formula One and a friend of the Stewarts. Recalling that Paul had expressed a wish to play a ukulele, Harrison had brought one along as a gift. His arrival through the back of the garage had been typically low-key but his presence quickly multiplied the gathering of photographers and television crews at the front door. As the cameras homed in, Ford's Martin Whitaker drily observed that the team was gaining more publicity by having the cars stay in the garage.

The only consolation was that Friday's times did not count towards grid positions. Nonetheless, there was much work to be done before the next free practice session the following morning and the all-important sixty-minute qualifying session in the afternoon. The first task was to establish precisely what had gone wrong.

Life was difficult enough, since this was the first time the Stewart-Ford team had been able to run (albeit briefly) two cars on the track at the same time. In addition, it was the first time that Magnussen's car had turned a wheel, the building of chassis number three having been completed in the garage once the mechanics had arrived in Melbourne at the beginning of the week. Under the circumstances, it was no surprise to find that the first practice session had been severely disrupted by mechanical glitches.

The Brazilian was twenty-first fastest of the twenty-four entries. He had managed just one timed lap

The problems were connected with the electronics controlling the gearbox, and a shortcoming with hydraulic seals in the gear shift actuator, faults which would have been ironed out had the team been able to complete harder and more lengthy running during testing. Now they needed to be sorted during a race weekend when there were not enough hours in the day.

This was only the first day and already the mechanics had barely seen their beds. At 5.30 p.m. on Friday Alan Maybin emerged from beneath Barrichello's car and headed for the massive fridge at the back of the garage. His peaked hat was on back to front, his white shirt splattered with oil and grease. As he pulled on a carton of soft drink, his weary look was replicated elsewhere as the mechanics showed signs of having had very little sleep. But no one was complaining.

'It's hard,' agreed Maybin, 'but everyone in here knew it was going to be difficult. It's the name of the game, particularly with a new team. The important thing is that the atmosphere is very good. We've got people here who've won races with other teams, so they know what it takes. Everyone is pulling together; there are no splinter groups, which you sometimes get inside teams. And it's very encouraging to see the reaction when people stop at the garage doors and look in.' Then he paused and threw the empty carton in the bin. 'We'll be all right,' he said quietly before heading back to a car which was literally split into a thousand pieces.

The mechanics finished work sometime after midnight. Alan Jenkins had been on his feet ever since his arrival on Wednesday morning. 'We were having a chat earlier in the evening,' said Le Fleming, 'and old AJ fell asleep mid-sentence, woke up a few minutes later – and carried on!' They tumbled into their beds shortly before 2 a.m. and were back at the track before dawn had broken on Saturday morning. 'We're arriving in the dark in more ways than one,' said Jenkins, a wry grin backing up the Liverpudlian humour.

It was 7 a.m. as the team-members emerged from the minibuses in the circuit car park, the personal identification cards slung round their necks allowing admission through the computerized turnstiles at the back of a paddock that was strangely subdued, thanks to the absence of engine noise and a blaring public address system. The drivers and the Stewarts, having done their bit at the Grand Prix Ball the previous evening before either leaving to eat quietly or attend some other function, arrived at 8 a.m. The unspoken question was: 'Have the problems been solved?'

Sixteen laps for Barrichello and twenty-one for Magnussen in the

'Alan Jenkins fell asleep mid-sentence, woke up a few minutes later – and carried on!'

morning session suggests that they have, although fifteenth for Rubens on the time sheet is just about where they should expect to be. He is having trouble with the gearbox occasionally shifting down one gear too many, but fortunately the problem has not occurred when he is running quickly. With all the technology incorporated in the electrics and hydraulics, there is no way the gearbox should do such a thing. But the uncomfortable fact is that it does. Barrichello's feedback is impressing Jenkins.

'You can do something with the engine and at the same time change something else on the car and Rubens can separate them out while driving quickly and tell you what you need to know afterwards,' said Jenkins. 'The first three minutes or so when he's talking are very good. But Rubens doesn't like sitting around talking about it all night. That's fair enough because sometimes you can talk yourself away from the main cause of the problem. It's like having a road accident and giving your impressions immediately afterwards. Fill out a form three days later, and it's as though you are talking about a different accident.'

Jan is twenty-first fastest and a little disappointed to be that far back. In a similar fashion to the previous day, he had locked his brakes excessively. The fault seemed to be with the driver rather than the car. **The impression is that he was trying too hard – or 'overdriving'.** But there is no time to go into great detail. The team is still finding its feet, nowhere near enough work having been done as the qualifying session approaches. It's too late now.

Both cars are set up for quick laps based on the small amount of accumulated knowledge they have. Assuming the machinery holds together, there is the hope that Rubens will qualify in the middle of the grid, with Jan not far behind. That view is obviously widespread as the media continues to make the trek to the bottom of the pit lane.

During the lunch break, two photographers work the Minardi garage on one side: no one bothers with Lola on the other. Meanwhile fifteen photographers and two television crews are focused on the immaculately run garage in the middle. It is difficult to tell whether they have come to record some noteworthy achievement or a high-profile new arrival falling flat on its face. As temperatures rise, it is clear that this will be the first stiff test for Stewart Grand Prix.

At 1 p.m. precisely, a green light marks the beginning of qualifying. No one ventures out. The feeling of anticlimax is emphasized by a comparatively silent pit lane. With each driver limited to twelve laps, there is no need to hurry. The chances are that the track will get quicker as the sixty minutes tick by and more rubber is laid down. By 1.15 p.m., most competitors have completed one flying lap, using one set of tyres to learn about the latest condition of the track.

Five minutes later Magnussen, who has been sitting in his car for some time, is the first to leave the Stewart pit. He registers a lap of 1m 34.623s. That makes him fourteenth overall. Two minutes later, Barrichello records 1m 34.978s. He is eighteenth. His next quick lap reduces his time to 1m 34.059s, good enough for fourteenth. Magnussen, meanwhile, has slipped to seventeenth fastest as other drivers improve. By 1.30 p.m. the pace has begun to pick up, Jacques Villeneuve setting the fastest time so far with a lap of 1m 29.369s. The Stewart team will never match that. But Barrichello is convinced there is more to come. He leaves the pit lane to start his second run.

Jackie and Paul Stewart spend their time between the pit wall and the garage. At each location there is a timing monitor. Barrichello's mechanics gather round the screen in the garage. The figures show each lap split into three sections. The figures are in white, unless a driver has gone faster than his previous personal best for this session, when they are shown in green. And if he is faster than everyone else, then they are shown in pink. That's the equivalent of the qualifying jackpot. It's also something for the future as far as the Stewart-Ford team is concerned.

Barrichello completes his run out of the pits and sets off on the flying lap. Being a midfield runner and therefore not of much interest to the television producer at a time when the big names are circulating, Barrichello will not be shown on the TV screen. He is therefore out of sight to the team, driving his heart out on everyone's behalf. There is nothing the mechanics and engineers can do now except watch the monitor and wait.

The figures from the first third of the lap are green. He's going for it. Barrichello reaches the timing beam at the end of the second section. Green again! Come on, Ruby. Keep it up. The final third will finish as he crosses the start/finish line. The crew-members watch the exit of the final corner, waiting for the white car to slide into view.

Here he comes. He looks quick; the engine is singing to its maximum as he accelerates through the gears, heading towards the line. Eyes back to the monitor.

There is nothing the mechanics and engineers can do now except watch the monitor and wait

Green! 1m 33.075s. It's worth tenth place! The team can hardly believe it. And he has two more sets of tyres left with time remaining for two more runs.

Barrichello knows the score as he hurtles back into the pit lane; the car is pushed back into the garage and quickly raised on the jacks in preparation for the change of tyres. There is a crisp urgency about every movement which shouts out: 'We're in business!'

Off the jacks, the engine blasts into life once more, away goes Barrichello down the pit lane. Anything seems possible, even though the track is now teeming with cars as drivers attempt to move further up the grid as the qualifying session enters its final phase. Barrichello completes his out lap and hammers across the line. Back to the monitor.

It seems to take him for ever to reach the first split point. Can he do it? How much has he got left? Will he get held up by a slower car? All these thoughts. Come on, where is . . .

It's worth tenth place! The team can hardly believe it

Green!

He's flying. Unbelievable. It seems too good to be true. It is.

A red flashing light at the bottom of the screen indicates that the red flag is out. The session has been stopped with immediate effect. Rubens finds out the reason why when he comes across the damaged remains of Nicola Larini's Sauber after the Italian had spun off. Barrichello cannot avoid running over a small piece of wreckage. He returns to the pits, hoping to have the last set of tyres fitted. The stopwatch says there will be enough time remaining for one more quick lap. The mechanics say he will be going nowhere, the piece of wreckage having damaged the underneath of the car.

All that can be done is wait and watch as the entire pit lane seems to decant onto the track once the green light comes on for the final few minutes. Gerhard Berger improves, knocking Rubens back to eleventh. No matter. It's a brilliant achievement in such illustrious company.

The Stewarts are elated – an outlet for the emotion which has been building for months – and feel sheer relief at having both cars qualify for the race. As Rubens climbs from the cockpit, he is embraced by Paul and Jackie. The media descend en masse to record the moment. Villeneuve may have taken pole position, but this is the human-interest story of the day.

It is also typical of motor racing, the juxtaposition of the Stewart garage and the teams around it telling about the highs and lows of this incredibly fickle business. The Lola garage has come to a standstill. Neither driver has qualified and the intensity of the effort to get the new team on the road is suddenly telling as fatigue overcomes the handful of crew-members. Meanwhile, two garages in the opposite direction, Damon Hill, the reigning world champion, the man who had started from the front of the grid for this race the previous year, has qualified by the skin of his teeth. Not that the Stewart team care too much about that.

'I'm thrilled, just thrilled,' says Jackie. 'We could have been in the top ten and I'm disappointed for Rubens because it wasn't his fault that we didn't.'

Barrichello grins. 'Close,' he says. 'I let you off this time.' Then he points to his wrist. Stewart knows what Rubens means. Barrichello had mentioned to Paul in passing how much he admired the Rolex Daytona watch. There is a three-year waiting list and, as a result, they are changing hands for as much as £6,000 in England. After much banter, Jackie had promised that if Rubens qualified inside the top ten in Melbourne, he would give him one. Stewart says he will extend the offer. A repeat of the thrill they have just experienced will make it worthwhile. Barrichello is totally convinced the watch will be his before long.

It was a sign of his maturity that Barrichello had refused to be rushed while sorting his car for that qualifying session. He remembered the previous year at Melbourne while driving for Jordan. 'We had been slower than expected in qualifying and we made changes which didn't work,' he recalls. 'This time, we thought the whole thing through. Then we made one big change and the car was perfect; just the way I want it. I was on a really quick lap at the end. I was running behind Villeneuve and suddenly, he went left. That's when I saw Larini for the first time. There was nothing I could do.'

In the midst of the excitement, it was easy to forget Magnussen as he climbed quietly from his car, disappointed about having been unable to better nineteenth place. His qualifying had been disrupted by a broken hose clip which sprayed water over the rear tyres. This was the first sign that the bad luck which had visited him during testing was not about to let up now that the season had started. Once repairs had been made, Jan rejoined moments before Larini had his accident. He went out again with everyone else for that final minute but never had a chance on such a crowded track.

'Jan has done a terrific job,' said Paul. 'He had to contend with that problem and we feel sure he would have improved on what was already a very

'We could have been in the top ten and I'm disappointed for Rubens because it wasn't his fault'

respectable performance.' At that moment, there seemed no reason to disagree with Stewart's assessment.

As the excitement continued to bubble among sponsors and guests on the small lawn by the back door the mechanics were facing reality and preparing for the next, more important stage. The two race cars would be stripped down and checked thoroughly as a matter of routine. They would require fresh engines. The gearboxes would be examined in great detail, the suspension components crack-tested. On top of that, Rubens' chassis needed repair work thanks to the damage caused by the debris. And the spare car, which might be needed on race day, required finishing off. The crew settled in for a long night.

And a long day. They never got to bed. There was time to go back to the hotel for a shower at 6.15 a.m. and then return in a clean uniform in time to finish off in readiness for the race warm-up at 9.30 a.m. Although the race was not due to start until 2 p.m., holding the warm-up at such an advanced hour would allow time for final preparations – but hopefully no accident repairs.

Jackie and Paul arrive before 8.30 a.m. in time for a team photograph in the pit lane. The race crew is fifty-seven strong. Each of the three cars has three mechanics and an engineer. There is a chief mechanic and a chief engineer who oversee the race cars. Alan Jenkins is in overall charge of the technical side, liaising with six engineers from Ford and Cosworth (led this weekend by Jim Brett), a technical coordinator (Andy Miller), spares coordinators, a hydraulics expert, engineers specializing in the gearboxes, five electronics experts from Ford, an aerodynamicist, fabricators, the five mechanics taking care of the tyres and fuel, plus the catering staff, Stuart Sykes and Sabine Marcon handling media requirements for Stewart and Ford respectively, and the PR team to make sure the sponsors and their guests have a smooth passage through the weekend.

The latter is a full-time job as thirty guests from Sanyo are located above the pits, sixty clients from Hertz are in a hospitality area near the lake at the rear of the circuit, a hundred Hewlett-Packard guests will be in one of the pit-straight grandstands, along with two hundred guests of Ford, HSBC and Highland Spring seated in the stands at Turn 4. As usual, there are insufficient passes to allow Paul and Jackie to bring all of their more important partners into the pits (a problem widespread in Formula One and not unique

They never got to bed
– there was time to go
back to the hotel for
a shower at 6.15 a.m.
and then return in a
clean uniform

to Stewart). But, typically, the Stewarts have planned to visit every location at some point during the weekend.

Naturally, the most common question concerns their expectations for the race. The answer is always the same because it is the only reasonable reply: they hope to finish. To do so at the end of ninety minutes' flat-out racing would be a major achievement for a new team. It would matter little which position they were credited with on the final leader board. Just so long as they were on it.

The sponsors get a chance to see 'their' drivers as Barrichello and Magnussen take part in a parade in open-topped cars. Then they disappear into the temporary room erected at the back of the garage, where they will eat pasta, make final plans about pit stop tactics with Jenkins and their engineers and then get some rest. As the drivers try to wind down, the rest of Albert Park is reaching an orchestrated pitch of excitement.

With the cars ready to roll, the mechanics move among the boxes stacked behind their work area and change into flameproof overalls. This is the next test. They have practised pit stops and refuelling at the factory. But it has not been enough. There is nothing to match the almost desperate urgency provided by the noise and clamour of the race itself. Teams such as Benetton will have been through the routine more than a thousand times over the winter. The boys from Stewart wish they could have done half that number. Too late now. Their best will have to be good enough.

Paul and Jackie appear in their white flameproof suits, Jackie retaining the tartan identity with his flat cap. The cars leave the pits. Jackie and Paul walk to the starting grid for the first time. There must have been times during the previous twelve months when they never thought this moment would happen. But there they are: one immaculate Stewart-Ford alongside Ralf Schumacher's Jordan on the sixth row of the grid; the other sharing the tenth row with the world champion. But not for long. As the cars set off on the final parade lap, Hill's Arrows breaks down. Already Stewart-Ford are looking good compared to this shambles. And the field is about to thin itself out even more.

Villeneuve makes a poor start from pole position and, on the rush to the first corner, Irvine's Ferrari dives on one side of the Williams, Herbert's Sauber on the other. There is not enough room for all three cars to run side by side through the right-hander. They collide. All three fail to complete the first lap.

Barrichello, seeing the dust and the chaos ahead of him, applies caution

There is nothing to match the almost desperate urgency provided by the noise and clamour of the race itself

and emerges in eleventh place. Magnussen, having made a good start, is thirteenth. They both move up one place when Ralf Schumacher makes a mistake on the next lap. By the end of lap four, they are ninth and eleventh, Magnussen moving into position behind his team-mate when the Jordan of Fisichella spins off on lap fifteen. At the same time, pulses are quickening in the Stewart garage as the pit stops draw near.

Magnussen is called in first. The mechanics go to work, each action measured and calm. There is no point in trying any heroics at the first attempt. All four wheels are changed, the refuelling hose is withdrawn, the car is dropped from the jacks, and Jan is waved out. With a crescendo of revs, he is gone. Perfect. The time taken, from the moment he entered the pit lane until he rejoined, was two seconds longer than Frentzen's stop in the leading Williams. No matter. It has been a very acceptable effort. Far better that than a fumble which could double the time.

It boosts confidence as the mechanics wait for Barrichello to take his turn. They trim half a second off Magnussen's time. As the race settles down again, the Stewart-Fords are handily positioned in ninth and tenth. They have just moved up one more place (thanks, unbelievably, to Alesi having run out of fuel after failing to stop when instructed by the Benetton team) when Magnussen hits trouble.

The next question is obvious: will Barrichello's car suffer a similar fate?

He makes his second refuelling stop as planned on lap thirty-five but, for some time now, he has been unhappy about the handling of the car. It was fine in the early stages of the race but, bit by bit, it began to feel bad. He completes one more lap before coming in for good. The right-rear suspension is found to have buckled.

It is difficult to tell the precise reason. The problem has not arisen before, mainly because the SF-1 has never done forty laps continuously until now. Investigation will reveal that a build-up in temperature (from the exhaust) has caused the suspension to weaken. In the meantime, the next question is obvious. Will Barrichello's car suffer a similar fate?

The answer is that it probably will, although Rubens should feel the handling start to go awry in the manner experienced by Magnussen. Besides, he is coping with another problem. He made his second stop without drama but reported that the oil light was on, a warning which matched the telemetry readings in the pits. There was little anyone could do. He was instructed to keep going and try and bring the car home.

With ten laps to go, he is in eighth place. Bearing in mind the possibility of a suspension problem, the difficult question remains: should they call him in? An engineer reports that he checked Rubens' car at the last pit stop and the suspension had seemed to be OK. Even so . . .

Almost immediately, the decision is made for the team as Barrichello's voice comes on the radio. 'The engine's gone. I'm stopped.' The Stewart-Ford is within twenty-five miles of the finish as it coasts onto the infield. The crew begin to peel off their flameproof gear and think about packing everything away. Suddenly, the lurking feeling of tiredness becomes overwhelming. As the race runs its course, with David Coulthard the surprise winner for McLaren, the two fellow Scots at the far end of the pit lane feel there is not much to celebrate. It is a natural reaction after coming so close to a finish on a day when more than half of the field had retired.

As the British national anthem rings out, there is little conversation in the Stewart garage, only noise and clatter as the boxes are readied to receive the massive amount of gear. The Ford and Cosworth technicians are studying the telemetry readouts. Paul and Jackie are in a huddle with Alan Jenkins. It does not take a genius to work out the topic of conversation in both camps, the suspension failure being the more worrying of the two reasons for retirement.

With business done for the day, the crowd has been allowed to venture onto the track. There is a strong contingent by the pit wall, calling for Jackie to break off his discussion. He moves across, signs autographs and receives enthusiastic comments from the fans. That helps to put things in perspective. The Stewart-Ford team have done themselves proud but, when working close to the action, it is difficult to see it that way.

'It's bitter-sweet,' says Jackie. 'I find it very difficult as an entrant. When you are a driver, it's easier because you have done your best. If the car stops, then it's usually not your fault. Even though I know that things can go wrong in the final ten laps, this has been difficult to take. I just wish we had been able to finish, if only for the team. Everyone has put so much into it. It would have been very nice to bring the car home.

'But these guys are right,' he says, waving a hand at the fans watching from the pit wall. 'I can't be too disappointed because there have been so many positive signs for the team that have come out of this weekend. It really has given us something to build on for the season ahead.'

Stack 'em high.
Bridgestones:
ready to roll.

ABOVE. Time for pit stop practice.

OPPOSITE. Dressed for action. Wearing his flameproof gear on race day, Jackie checks progress on the monitors at the garage entrance.

BELOW. The Stewarts and their drivers keep an eye on the opposition from the pit wall during practice.

RIGHT. The windowless
office with its temporary
partitions was the only
source of privacy in the
Stewart garage.
BELOW. Popular as ever.
Jackie obliges a marshal
in the pit lane at
Melbourne.

LEFT. Rubens waits to climb aboard while final preparations are made. BELOW. Too good to be true. A Stewart-Ford, eleventh on the grid for the first race.

ABOVE. Magnussen got off to a shaky start.

RIGHT. Team work. The refuelling crew wait for their big moment during the race.

CHAPTER NINE

SOUTH AMERICA TO
SAN MARINO

THERE WAS A GAP OF THREE WEEKS between Melbourne and the next race, in Brazil. The team required every spare minute as they made routine preparations in between addressing the problem with the rear suspension.

On paper, it did not look good. The media tended to give the simple fact that the suspension had failed, but without going into the detail which would explain why. That was a fact which Jenkins and his engineers had to live with, the simple answer being to ensure that the failure did not occur again. Unfortunately, by curing that problem they created another which was even more spectacular than the first. During a test session at Silverstone, the rear wing fell off Magnussen's car.

The trade press carried photographs of the SF-1 trailing into the pit lane with a major part of its familiar profile missing. In this case, the pictures said a thousand words which the team did not wish to read. The reason for the failure was soon established. But that would do little to appease the growing belief among casual observers that the team was struggling to make the grade; that this business of racing in Formula One might be proving too much.

It was true that the Stewarts had a lot on their plate. Quality time with their families and friends was almost unknown. During one of the so-called free weekends between Grands Prix, Jackie and Paul were at Donington Park to watch the progress of the Paul Stewart Racing entries in the opening rounds of the Formula Three and Formula Vauxhall championships. The formulas embraced by the company as a whole were as varied as you could wish for but professionalism remained the watchword in them all. PSR drivers won their respective races and at least provided a brief distraction from the niggling technical worries afflicting the Formula One effort.

The problem in Australia turned out to be as suspected during initial inspection in the pit lane in Melbourne. The exhaust gases had been playing on a leg of the top wishbone on the rear suspension. During the course of more than 120 miles of hard motoring – a distance never before covered without stopping – the material had been softened by the gradual build-up of heat. There had been no hint of the problem before. Yet, to the layman, it looked nothing more than a silly oversight.

'The exhaust outlet position is a very sensitive issue,' said Jenkins. 'The engine requirements for the correct tuned length are competing for packaging space with the rear suspension, wing and bodywork. We had quite complex

During a test session at Silverstone, the rear wing fell off Magnussen's car

heat shields in place but really they turned out to give a false feeling of security because they were hiding the problem. So we made a decision to change the exhaust layout and then test it at Silverstone.'

During the test, a bracket attaching the exhaust to the undertray broke. The angle of the pipe changed slightly and allowed the hot gases to blast the lower support for the rear wing, reducing the strength and very quickly causing the complete aerofoil to fly off. The good news was that the team had been able to identify the problem instantly. It would never occur again. But that was of little interest to rivals keen to knock a team which, on the evidence of Australia alone, was clearly going places. From a more practical point of view, it was more work for the workshop personnel as they prepared for the long haul to South America and races in Brazil and Argentina. Somehow, David Stubbs managed to have everything ready in time.

'The business with the wing didn't cause any major problems,' said the team manager. 'OK, it was something we had not bargained for, but we were able to react to it. Immediately after the test, we had a night, a full day and another night to get everything ready for shipment. All the boxes, complete with drawers and so on, had finally arrived and that made life more straightforward. Instead of dumping bits and pieces in massive boxes and hoping for the best, everything was in its proper place. The pack-up went very well. I finished at 12.30 a.m., whereas with the first one I left the factory at 9.30 the following morning!'

It was to be a sign of how the entire operation was becoming more integrated. The working area in the garages at Interlagos in Brazil were cramped and difficult, but the team settled in quickly and began preparations for practice. Instead of dealing with each incident and emergency as it arose and hoping for the best there would actually be a plan of attack when it came to setting up the car for qualifying and the race. Barrichello qualified eleventh with Magnussen taking twentieth. It was almost a repeat of Australia but the circumstances were quite different.

'In Australia, the car was OK but we weren't really on top of it,' says Jenkins. 'You could almost say that in Melbourne Rubens out-qualified the car. The problem was the sheer amount of work we had to get through. It was murder. We could have done a bit better with the car set-up. Rubens actually carried it because he was confident enough to push the car as hard as it would go even though it wasn't handling the way he wanted.

It was to be a sign of how the entire operation was becoming more integrated

141 ●

'In Brazil, it was the other way round. I think the car was better than qualifying suggested. This was the first time that we were able to start forming judgements of where we were compared to the other teams. To be perfectly honest, within or just outside the top ten in qualifying is where we wanted to be; I wouldn't have been very happy if we had been further back than that.

'Brazil was a pretty good test because the Interlagos track is quite an interesting mixture; there are slow bits and busy bits and some areas – such as the long climb towards the pit straight – where horsepower is everything. The good thing was that Rubens was actually pretty pleased with the car in Brazil, more so than in Australia, and in that sense we expected to be higher up the grid. The split times showed that we were pretty reasonable when it came to making the chassis and tyres work. Although it was certainly possible to improve the car for certain parts of the circuit, the major problem seemed to be acceleration onto the long straight – but that's not to say that the other parts of the car could not have been better as well.

'We had been consistently inside the top ten during free practice but we were not on the ball enough during qualifying to see that there were some clouds coming in and that it would be cooler (and the track faster) during the last seven or eight minutes. Eleventh wasn't bad for our second race – but we expected better.'

Jenkins was perhaps being too critical of himself and the team. Examination of the lap times showed that the cars were bunched closer than ever before, a mere half a second covering the drivers between fifth and twelfth places on the grid. It was no shame to be eleventh in this company and, more to the point, the car and engine had run reasonably consistently without a series of unexpected dramas. Nothing, however, is straightforward in Formula One.

'There was one thing which drove us mad,' admits Jenkins. 'It seemed that every time we went to fire up the engine, it wouldn't start. We also had a problem with the crankshaft oil seals. We would come in first thing in the morning, and once we got the engine running there would be oil all over the floor in a matter of moments. We had to set to work with Cosworth and find out why this was happening. By working through problems with the car's oil system, the r.p.m. of the starter assembly and details in the engine, we finally got to the bottom of a problem which would have been sorted out earlier if we had been able to do more testing.

'Brazil was a pretty good test because the Interlagos track is quite an interesting mixture'

● 142

'Overall, however, we seemed to be getting better and better. We were beginning to learn about how to get the best out of the tyres. There seemed to be more time to think things through. In Melbourne, for example, I remember sitting down after the warm-up had finished on Sunday morning and then thinking, "What are we going to do for the race?" We were working things out as we went along. In the end, it was almost a case of putting fuel in the car and then trying to stay awake! But in Brazil everything seem to be much more orderly. Until the start of the race.'

As Barrichello reached his place on the grid for the start proper, the engine electronics prematurely prompted the throttle to call for maximum revs. Barrichello had no option but to switch off the engine. As the field roared off, his race seemed to be over. In fact, with the Stewart-Ford stranded on the track, just over the brow of the hill leading onto the very fast pit straight, and with no means of removing the stricken car thanks to concrete walls on either side, the race director had no option but to show the red flag. It would give Barrichello the chance to take the restart in the spare car but the reprieve would come too late for the hapless Magnussen, an innocent victim of a multi-car collision at the first corner.

Barrichello duly started the race but his home event would last for a mere sixteen laps before a rear toe-link bracket came loose. Jenkins had been paying special attention to this area and new parts had been fitted for the race. The retirement was due to manufacturing problems rather than a surprise structural failure. Nonetheless, it was not what the team needed in the light of previous problems in this area.

The statistics may have shown two races and two retirements but at least the team was still able to take part. Lola, after failing to qualify for their first race in Australia, had not made the trip to Brazil. The company, highly respected in other branches of motor sport, had been brought to the brink of bankruptcy by its efforts to make the final step to Formula One. If nothing else, Lola's abysmal failure highlighted the worth of the other Formula One debutant.

Stewart Grand Prix had every reason to feel optimistic about the next race in Argentina. More than that, the mechanics and engineers had actually managed to have a decent night's sleep at the end of each day. And now the travelling team was due for a few days off in Buenos Aires while waiting for the freight to be shipped from Brazil. David Stubbs, meanwhile, had returned

It was not what the team needed in the light of previous manufacturing problems

to Milton Keynes with Alan Jenkins, their baggage augmented with suitcases filled with parts requiring modification.

Paul took the opportunity to visit an old friend, Nando Parrado, in Uruguay before setting out on a special mission with his father. In the company of Constancio Vigil, a South American media mogul, they flew by private plane to Balcarce, a small town of no particular note other than the fact that it had been the home of arguably one of the greatest racing drivers the world has ever seen.

Juan Manuel Fangio won the world championship five times, a record which is unbeaten. Fangio remained a model of dignity and diplomacy, even after his retirement from the cockpit in 1958. He was, and is, one of Jackie Stewart's few heroes, someone to be greatly admired. Stewart was deeply honoured when asked to be one of the pall-bearers at the great man's funeral in 1995. 'Carrying Fangio to his resting place,' says Jackie, 'was one of the most important things of my life.' The private visit with Paul to the family crypt brought those memories flooding back. It also strengthened their resolve to produce the sort of professional operation of which Fangio would have approved.

Certainly, he would have been impressed by the team's performance on the first day of practice at the Buenos Aires autodrome, in a suburban park just thirty minutes' drive from the centre of this splendid city. Time spent working progressively through various suspension and aerodynamic set-ups on the SF-1 saw Barrichello establish second fastest time, with Magnussen taking fifteenth place. It was true that the times meant nothing in terms of grid positions – these would be decided as usual during qualifying on Saturday – but the performance sent morale soaring sky-high.

'The car is incredibly good,' said Barrichello. 'This track is tight, with lots of corners, and my car is coming out of the corners fast – that's what Argentina is all about!'

Apart from Barrichello's obvious statement of intent on the track, Magnussen had been able to complete his maximum of thirty laps without interruption for the first time.

'The team deserves this,' said Jackie. 'Everyone has worked so hard. I'm thrilled.'

Those would not be the words which would spring to mind as Stewart waited for qualifying to commence twenty-three hours later.

> **They flew by private plane to Balcarce, the home of arguably one of the greatest racing drivers**

Trouble had started on Saturday morning when the engine failed, almost without warning, on Magnussen's car. During the course of this drama, the oil had caught fire and overheated part of the gearbox hydraulics as the car sat out on the circuit. The marshals had played safe and liberally doused the rear of the SF-1 in extinguisher powder, thus giving the mechanics a huge mess to clear up once the car had been returned to the garage. With insufficient time to change the heat-affected components, it was decided to gamble that they had not been harmed unduly. In fact the heat had been enough to create an airlock in the hydraulic pump, which meant great difficulty in persuading the replacement engine to run. With qualifying looming, it was decided to let Magnussen have use of the spare car.

Meanwhile Barrichello was preparing himself for what looked like being a superb effort. As he made ready to climb aboard his car the engine was started. A valve suddenly jammed open and allowed oil – now under huge pressure – to be pumped to places it had no right to be. There was a moment's disbelief all round as the crew stared at the floor awash with black liquid. Now both drivers would need the spare car. Fortunately, that seemed to be working OK even though it would not be set up to the full satisfaction of either driver.

'So there we were,' recalls Jenkins, 'more competitive than we had ever been – and the whole thing had suddenly turned to you-know-what. For a terrible moment it seemed we might be pushed to get either car to qualify. The thing to do was take Rubens to one side and tell him not to worry. Say something like: "Go out and set a time in the spare car, and even if we can get your race car ready for just ten minutes at the end then you will definitely qualify in the top six." We told him to think about that.

'Jan went out and did a lap, then Rubens took the spare car for one run. Fortunately, because both drivers are of a similar build, it meant the changeover was fairly straightforward when it came to adjusting belts and pedals and so on. Meanwhile, the sticking valve had responded. We had shut everything down, started again and that allowed the valve to reseat itself. It was fine after that. Meanwhile, we had a huge oil slick on the garage floor to tidy up . . . '

Barrichello was able to manage two runs in his race car. The final one was a brilliant effort, good enough for fifth place. As he returned to the pits and a rapturous welcome from the crew, Barrichello removed his old wristwatch and tossed it out of the cockpit. Jackie was more than happy to organize the supply, as promised, of a more expensive replacement. Magnussen, meanwhile,

The final run was a brilliant effort, good enough for fifth place

had taken fifteenth place; a creditable performance considering the Dane's lack of running – but disappointing in the company of such excellence.

The weather conditions that evening were idyllic. With no wind, the late afternoon sun cast an orange glow along the pit lane. The front doors of the Stewart garage were wide open, the blast of music from the team's sound system declaring the upbeat mood. All the signs were good.

'We thought that Rubens might have been a bit down after the disappointment in his home race,' said Andy Le Fleming. 'But he has stayed calm and been very positive all the way. Even during the drama at the start of qualifying. That sort of thing helps everyone. Everything about the team is a bit tighter and working that bit better.'

Jenkins agreed. 'I've returned to England in between the races and I've noticed the difference each time I come back. There has been a step up in the calmness and organization each time, a really incredible ramping up on the organizational and team side of things in these three races.'

As he spoke, the mood was relaxed in the broad alleyway between the back of the garages and the office blocks housing team management. Taking advantage of the shade, Jackie and Paul sat on packing cases and gave interviews as they assessed the latest position of the team.

'The launch of the Stewart-Ford had been our high point,' said Jackie. 'But this is fantastic, really wonderful. The mechanics and engineers were working under a lot of pressure because of all those problems and they did a tremendous job coping with all the changing of cars and so on at the beginning of qualifying. Obviously the Bridgestone tyres are giving us an advantage, but it's also clear that the chassis is working well because this is not an out-and-out power circuit. I'm particularly pleased for Jan, qualifying fifteenth despite so little running, none of which was his fault.'

Luck never fails to play its part and the team had to hope that only good fortune would come their way on Sunday 13 April. Certainly everything went according to plan during the warm-up on race morning, Barrichello setting third fastest time as different tactics were explored. The run to the first corner, however, would be more uncertain in such competitive company. Filling the front row, the Williams-Renaults of Villeneuve and Frentzen. Ahead of Barrichello, Olivier Panis and Michael Schumacher, with Michael's brother, Ralf, joining Rubens on row three. If Barrichello could at least maintain his position at the end of the first lap, he would be well placed to make the most of tyres which would serve him well during the remaining seventy-one laps.

As the field surged off the line on the short sprint to the first corner, a tight right-hander, Michael Schumacher found his helmet visor coated in oil sprayed from the back of Frentzen's Williams. Momentarily disorientated, Schumacher spun as he reached the corner – and took Barrichello with him.

The only good thing to be said was that Rubens had managed to keep his engine running and he used it to literally shovel the stalled Ferrari out of the way, plumes of smoke rising off the rear tyres as the Stewart acted as a battering ram in order to clear a path. Once rid of the Ferrari, Barrichello spun his car to face the correct direction, his next mission being the nursing of his car, complete with broken nose, to the pits.

Having seen the pictures on television and heard Barrichello's call on the radio, the pit crew prepared themselves for a change of nose-cone – a routine they had yet to try in anger. They were to get plenty of practice at it because at that moment Magnussen was running into the back of a Tyrrell at the end of the lap and he would require similar treatment. Fortunately, Jan would come in at the end of the following lap, thus avoiding overcrowding outside the door of the Stewart garage.

Barrichello was quickly attended to, the mechanics carrying out a swift replacement despite their lack of practice. Having suffered from someone else's mistake, Barrichello was at least able to make the most of the fact that the drama at the first corner (Coulthard had also been forced to abandon his car) had brought the race under the control of the Safety Car, thus allowing Rubens to speed round the lap and latch on to the tail of the slow-moving field.

When the Safety Car pulled in at the end of the fourth lap and the race was allowed to restart, Barrichello went to work, slicing through the backmarkers and working his way into eighth place before his first planned pit stop. 'I was really enjoying myself; it was the best car I've ever had,' Rubens would say afterwards. Unfortunately, it had yet to become the most reliable car.

On lap twenty-four his engine lost hydraulic pressure when a Moog valve fell apart, something which rarely happens. Magnussen, meanwhile, had soldiered on after his pit stop. He would last until lap sixty-six before the oil-pressure light blinked a warning to stop. Magnussen had gone far enough to be classified tenth, the first official finish – of sorts – for the Stewart-Ford team.

Magnussen had gone far enough to be classified tenth, the first official finish – of sorts – for the Stewart-Ford team

'A bit of a negative ending,' agreed Jackie, before adding brightly, 'but we've enjoyed a very positive weekend. I feel confident that Rubens could have had a podium finish. But, of course, there are no ifs in motor racing.'

Alan Jenkins was aware of that as he made his way towards the paddock exit, the early evening sun casting long shadows across the neighbouring park. 'Disappointing? Yes, I suppose it is,' he said quietly. 'There was nothing Rubens could do about the first corner.' Then the familiar wry grin. 'But it was good news/bad news again. Bad news that someone else should take him out; good news that he was running with Michael Schumacher when it happened!'

Carrying a bulging briefcase in one hand and a laundry bag with a change of clothes in the other, Jenkins was heading for the airport, glad that the three long-haul races were now over, the start of the European season bringing the promise of more organizational stability as the season began to get into its stride. It would allow the team to bring their transporters to each race. The convenience would be similar to throwing everything into the family saloon and motoring to a holiday destination rather than suffering the restrictions imposed by suitcases and flying.

'Disappointing?
Yes, I suppose it is,'
he said quietly

Stewart Grand Prix had three trucks, designed for the job in hand – one rigid-chassis and two articulated. All three would set off on the weekend before the San Marino Grand Prix since this race called for a reasonably long haul to Imola in northern Italy. The rigid vehicle, driven by Graham Civil, would form the advance party, leaving Milton Keynes on Saturday with garage equipment and the two refuelling rigs on board. The transporters would depart the following day in time to reach Calais on Sunday evening in readiness for an early start on Monday (French law forbids heavy transport to use the roads on Sunday).

Each articulated truck, costing £250,000, had a specific role. Gerrard O'Reilly and Michael Overy took charge of the support truck, a mini-factory on wheels with equipment on board ranging from toolboxes to lathes and milling machines. Paul Singlehurst and Julian Marlow shared the driving of the race truck carrying the three cars and spare parts covering everything from bodywork and floors to transmissions and suspension components. The engines and telemetry equipment would be brought separately on the articulated transporter belonging to Ford, John Cushing and Derek 'Del' Silver joining their Stewart colleagues for the journey south.

The convoy left Calais at 7.30 a.m. on Monday 21 April, the drivers taking four-hour stints at the wheel in between resting in the rear bunk or keeping in touch by radio on the run to the overnight halt at Chamonix. The optimistic mood established in Australia and South America continued even though O'Reilly's truck was without the benefit of music, the cassette player having packed up and the radio being inoperable. The main battery had been disconnected during a final inspection before leaving and O'Reilly did not have the code necessary to unlock the radio. A call to Milton Keynes on his GSM phone initiated the search. By 3 p.m. there was music, an accessory as vital to a truckie as diesel in his tank.

Each vehicle would require a daily 600-litre refill, plus, at the final stop along the route, a further 600 litres to feed the on-board generators in readiness for the supplying of essential power at the track. The crews' refuelling en route would be minimal, sandwiches grabbed in a service area, ensuring that Chamonix would be reached by early evening which would allow time for a proper meal and a few beers before bed.

It was a short journey at 8.00 on Tuesday morning to the Mont Blanc tunnel and the Italian border. Thanks to the EU, cross-border paperwork is no longer the nightmare it was, the most essential tools for the truck crews being team caps and T-shirts to ensure a quick check of the tell-tale tachograph in the cab and an easy passage. Failure to look after the customs officers could see them exercise their right to stop and search the truck, which could take all day if they felt inclined.

The final leg through Italy was tedious, not helped by the 80 k.p.h. speed limit. The trucks ran in line astern, other team transporters coming into view as they neared Imola; despite the intense rivalry on the track, there is a camaraderie among truckies which does not exist in any other branch of Grand Prix racing. As more than sixty vehicles – the team motorhomes and transporters joining the trucks from tyre companies and trade suppliers – gathered in the designated assembly area outside the circuit on Tuesday afternoon there was a resurgence of the 'new term' feeling as the crews compared notes and admired the latest and greatest in transport equipment commissioned by each team. Singlehurst and O'Reilly had nothing to be ashamed of as the immaculate white transporters with the tartan logos joined the ranks of their established rivals.

The paddock gates were opened at 5.30 p.m. Each team has its garages and parking spaces designated by Formula One Administration (FOA) and the strict

The most essential tools for the truck crews are team caps and T-shirts to ensure a quick check of the tell-tale tachograph

pecking order continued as the top teams were given the largest garages. Stewart was shoehorned into the top of the long paddock at the point where it narrowed to barely the size of a transporter, O'Reilly and Singlehurst having to use their HGV skills to the full as they backed their trucks into position. That done, the unpacking and setting-up process began.

Everything was ready for the arrival of the mechanics and team personnel during the course of the next two days. For the first time, the team would have use of their motorhome, which would be parked beside a similar luxury vehicle run by Ford. Stewart's motorhome would be for team management and for entertaining sponsors; Ford's would cater for their management personnel as well as doubling up as a watering hole for the press. This being the first race, however, Dave Stubbs found there were phone calls to be made as he chased up missing parts for the new awning which would run the length of the Stewart motorhome. Now that the team was operating in Europe, Stubbs also had to hold discussions with MSL, the catering company which would provide food each day for mechanics from most teams in a separate kitchen/eating area tucked away at the far end of the paddock.

The small office in a downstairs corner of the Ford motorhome would be used by Sabine Marcon and Stuart Sykes. A press release, produced each day for distribution in the media centre and transmission to Ford and Stewart associates worldwide, would tell the story of the team's progress. Once again, it would be good news/bad news.

Friday's release detailed an encouraging start as Barrichello set the eighth fastest time during free practice, with Magnussen sixteenth. Both drivers had worked on the handling of their cars, although at Imola everyone knew that engine power would be one of the dominant factors. Ford and Cosworth had been working hard to make ready the latest version of the Zetec-R engine, the Project 6. Tests had yet to show satisfactory reliability but maximum performance at Imola was so badly needed that an interim version was produced and examples of this engine would be given to each driver on Saturday.

That seemed to have been a sensible move as Barrichello and Magnussen continued to produce encouraging lap times, but as the Saturday morning session reached its conclusion the first problems with the latest engine emerged. Barrichello's initial run in qualifying was blighted by an engine misfire, forcing a switch to the spare car equipped with the older Project 5 engine. Magnussen did not have that luxury when he experienced a similar problem.

Tests had yet to show satisfactory reliability but maximum performance at Imola was badly needed

Instead of making the top ten, as hoped, Stewart had to be satisfied with thirteenth and sixteenth places on the grid, Barrichello leading as usual.

In the warm-up on race morning, the positions were reversed as Magnussen set seventh fastest time, a couple of tenths of a second ahead of his team-mate. No one was reading much into this, however, since the track had been wet and the lap times were not indicative of what might happen if the forecast for a dry race was correct. In fact as the start time approached the Stewart-Ford team felt they would be lucky to go racing at all.

Magnussen's engine was being warmed up when a valve inside the V10 suddenly misbehaved in an identical manner to the mishap in Argentina. Within seconds, fifteen litres of oil were sprayed all over Mr Stewart's immaculate garage just as Jackie was arriving through the back door, dressed in his flameproof overalls, ready to go racing.

'We told him it might be a good idea if he went back outside and thought about something else for a few minutes,' said Jenkins. 'The boys were on the problem immediately, so I thought I would get out of their way. There was this huge mess, and as I was backing out of the front of the garage I looked to one side and couldn't believe what I was seeing.

'There was fuel running everywhere from a hose on one of the refuelling rigs. We had been issued with new specification hoses and one of them had split as the tank was pressurized in readiness for the race. We stood there for a couple of seconds and stared. It was unbelievable. Carnage everywhere. But the guys were fantastic. They set to work without any fuss. They handled everything and we were out on the starting grid on time, with everything ready, just as if nothing had happened.'

The team deserved a decent result after all of that but the misfortunes were set to continue. Last-minute adjustments to Magnussen's car to compensate for the change from wet weather to dry meant the SF-1 was running too close to the ground. Magnussen found this out on the third lap as a particularly bad bump sent the car into a spin and retirement as he braked for the Acque Minerali chicane at the bottom of a steep section of track. Barrichello ran in the midfield for thirty-three laps before stopping with an oil-system related engine failure. That made it four races without a decent finish. The chances of breaking that duck at the next race on the car-breaking streets of Monte Carlo seemed remote. As the Stewart-Ford team could already testify, however, nothing in motor racing is ever clear-cut.

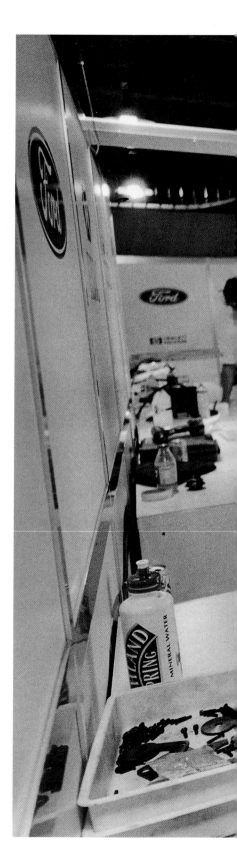

ABOVE. Organized chaos. Spare parts are stored in the limited space available at the back of the garage at Interlagos.

RIGHT. Fine tuning. Rubens receives a massage to help cope with the physical forces exerted by a Formula One car.

OPPOSITE. All aboard. The interior of the race truck: two cars on the lower deck, one on the upper. LEFT. Watching you watching me. Julian Marlow takes a photo as Michael Overy moves ahead en route to Imola. Gerrard O'Reilly has a break in the bunk. BELOW. Journey's end. The start of serious work in the Imola paddock as the first car rolls out.

ABOVE. Julian Marlow washes off the grime on arrival at Imola. RIGHT. Timely reward. Rubens receives his Rolex watch from Paul.

LEFT. The hurly-burly of qualifying.
BELOW. Can't wait. A Stewart-Ford accelerates onto the track at Imola. Judging by the tyre marks, one or two rivals have made more spectacular departures.

ABOVE. Magnussen gets down to business.

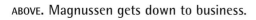

RIGHT. You don't want to do it that way, Rubens. The ITV studio team watch Barrichello slide onto a kerb during the warm-up on race day at Imola.

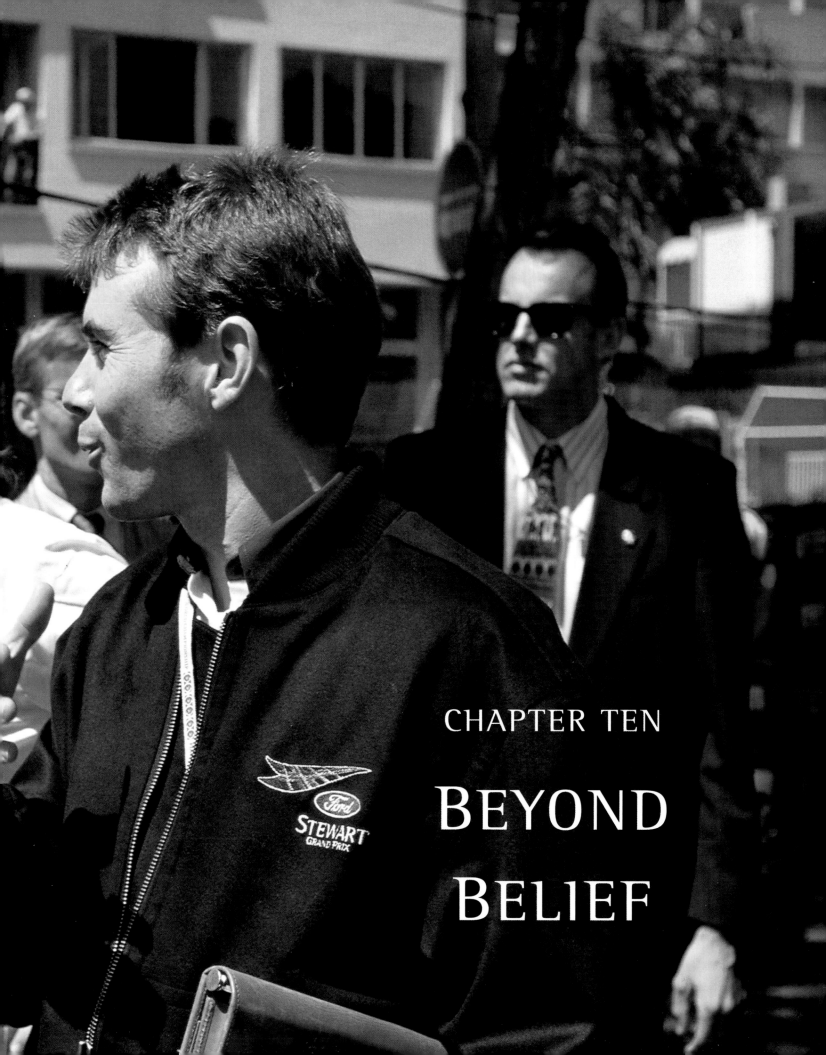

CHAPTER TEN

BEYOND
BELIEF

**JACKIE WAS SEEING MONTE CARLO FROM A DIFFERENT PERSPECTIVE.
He had been the most celebrated man in town after superb wins in 1966,
1971 and 1973, victory in the Monaco Grand Prix meriting a special place on
the CV of any racing driver. Now he was an entrant; a new boy without special
entitlement. Stewart was aware of that from the moment he arrived in the
principality.**

Working the Monaco Grand Prix is something to be endured by team personnel faced with the hindrances of a temporary circuit. But at least Stewart Grand
Prix were prepared for that. Old hands such as Alan Jenkins, Dave Redding
and Andy Le Fleming had been able to warn of the difficulties presented by
a paddock which was a good ten-minute walk from a cramped pit lane. Fetch
and carry would be the order of the day.

Dave Stubbs, having worked with Williams and Brabham in the past, knew
all about the hassle but his troubles began even before the transporters left
England. The Monaco race added another difficulty by holding the first day
of practice on Thursday, rather than Friday. That meant one day less in the
already brief turnaround period at the factory after the trucks had returned
from Imola. And now, for good measure, Stubbs learned that a proposed strike
by French lorry drivers threatened to close the motorway network completely
on the Monday of race week. There was no alternative but to leave Milton
Keynes earlier than planned, thus giving the team a matter of days to strip
down and prepare the cars and restock the transporters.

The two articulated trucks left England on Friday 2 May, arriving in Nice
on the following day. With the paddock not yet available, the trucks were
parked and the crews flew home, returning to Nice on Monday in order to
make the sixty-minute journey along the coast, park in the paddock and unload
in readiness for the arrival of team personnel on Tuesday.

Stubbs was not surprised to find that the Stewart trucks had been directed
to a secondary paddock located in a multi-storey car park. The top teams
had been given the prime spaces in the paddock on the quayside, but despite
the extra distance to travel the car park was at least out of the way and free
from the barely controlled chaos on the quay. Indeed, there would be no
need to erect the awnings on the sides of the transporters since they were
already parked under cover with plenty of room for the team to spread themselves out. Stubbs was not complaining about any of this. But he sensed there

**Stubbs learned that a
proposed strike by French
lorry drivers threatened
to close the motorway
network completely**

might be one or two protests when he learned about the fate of the team's motorhome.

The Monaco Grand Prix is motor racing's showcase and no one is better equipped than Jackie Stewart to exploit such a glittering asset. The stunning backdrop alone makes a lasting impression on any first-time visitor. Throw in the drama of twenty-two Formula One cars let loose on the streets and the picture is complete. The other benefit is that top-class hotels and restaurants are on site rather than in some town or city several miles distant from the racetrack. Monaco brings motor racing to the front door of an influential audience.

Yet, despite the immediacy of the expensive trappings, the motorhome would have an important part to play. It would represent the inner sanctum, a place where only the select few would be granted admission. Or at least it would if parked in its rightful place on the edge of the shimmering harbour.

The alarm bells started to ring when Stubbs was informed that the quayside paddock was full and the motorhome would have to reside with the transporters. He knew as well as anyone that executives representing the team's multinational partners had not come to Monte Carlo to view the inside of a concrete car park. Jackie did not take the news well. And the frustration turned to annoyance when he discovered that his was the only motorhome to have been eased out.

It was true that the quayside was indeed crowded, but although nobody on the Stewart team would say as much there seemed to be a touch of vindictiveness about such treatment. It was a hint of the petty jealousy which will surface in any business driven by ego and a ruthless competitiveness. The joke in the paddock was that by being parked halfway up the cliff face Jackie would be closer to the palace at the top.

Stewart would not deny his link with the Rainiers. In fact, he was very proud of it. Paul and Mark had gown up with the Rainier children and the Stewart family had been regular visitors, frequently at times other than during Grand Prix week. Each time Jackie returned to Monaco it was not as a retired racing driver and former winner but as someone with a long relationship with the principality. But even that would not get the motorhome shifted.

Accepting that there was no point in fighting the decision, Stewart at least had the use of the Ford motorhome, which had been granted a place overlooking the magnificent marina. Any aggravation had to be viewed as part of

The team's multinational partners had not come to Monte Carlo to view the inside of a concrete car park

the induction process. The first-year difficulties were bound to be many and varied, the locating of decent hotel rooms being typical. Particularly at Monaco. The mechanics had to make do with accommodation in Menton, the tortuous trip back and forth to the neighbouring district adding to an already long and tiring day.

Neither did it help that Stewart-Ford had been located at the bottom end of the pit lane, as far as it was possible to be from the paddock. This, however, brought a bonus in that the spare car and various bits and pieces could be stored in a rare piece of free space at the end of the pit block. Other teams, crammed in the middle of the pit lane, would not be so fortunate. Everyone had their problems. The track would be the great equalizer.

Barrichello had experience of the circuit, this being his fourth visit. Magnussen would have to find his way around while at the same time attempting to sort out his car, a difficult process since the slightest driving error would be punished by the waiting kerbs and metal barriers. Magnussen did well to have just one incident on the first day – and get away with it. Approaching the corner at the end of the main straight at 175 m.p.h., he felt the brakes begin to lock as he arrived too fast. Rather than attempt to get around the corner – and risk hitting the barrier – or brake extra hard and ruin a set of tyres for no good reason, he chose to shoot into the escape road.

His cool thinking was noted by everyone willing the Dane to produce the level of performance which his past record proved he was capable of. According to Jackie, however, the most recent part of his racing history – time spent racing powerful touring cars in the German championship – had led him into bad habits which were costing him time now that finesse, particularly when braking, meant everything. To that end, Jackie had spent a day with Jan and the PSR Formula Vauxhall drivers, Luciano Burti and Justin Wilson, comparing notes in a race-prepared Ford Escort rally car on the Oulton Park circuit in Cheshire. The comparative lap times, apart from proving Stewart's suspicions were correct as he sat beside Magnussen, showed that the former world champion had not lost his touch. With the exception of Alain Prost, no other team owner in the F1 pit lane was in a position to provide such practical help.

Barrichello, meanwhile, proved he was more than capable of looking after himself as he consistently set times in the top six during free practice. He finished the first day thirteenth on the time sheet thanks to his engine failing just as he was about to make the most of a track which was continually

> His cool thinking was noted by everyone willing the Dane to produce the level of performance he was capable of

picking up speed as rubber was laid on the racing line. As investigations continued into the problems experienced at Imola with the Project 6 engine, Ford and Cosworth had chosen to stay with the Project 5 version for a race in which reliability would be the criterion rather and out-and-out power.

'It's been quite satisfying,' said Alan Jenkins. 'This circuit represents another type of challenge for our car and it's good to see that the direction indicated in Argentina, where the car and the tyres could come into their own and pure power was not so critical, has turned out right again here.

'The other difference here, of course, is the working conditions everyone has to cope with. For the team's first go at Monaco, in the unique circumstances of having our garage so far away, the team have done well to escape from Alcatraz [the nickname given to the multi-storey car park] to the relative freedom of the pit lane and make everything function. It just shows how well they are working together. And now we have a free day on Friday to think about what we have learned so far.'

Formula One insiders view Friday in Monaco with scepticism. For some, the day off seems to allow nothing more than another opportunity for the Monegasque traders to extract more money from the visitors. For others, the free day is a rare chance to drift through the most charismatic paddock in the world, take in the sights and catch up on gossip. But for the unfortunate teams Friday is another crowded working day, albeit without the pressure of a strict timetable of track activity.

Paul and Jackie were involved in various meeting and press interviews before breaking off to join Helen and Victoria for lunch at a small café at Tabac, a name made famous by the corner it overlooks. The profile of the bend had changed in detail since the days when Jackie raced through the left-hander, but the essential challenge remained. The driver had to urge his car through this blind corner as quickly as possible knowing that placing a wheel no more than an inch out of line would spell instant retirement. Monaco may not have been about power and maximum speed, but it remained the ultimate test of precision and commitment.

After lunch, Paul made his way to the yacht club on the opposite side of the harbour, where HSH Prince Albert would attend an auction of motor racing memorabilia sold in the aid of charity. Steering wheels, bodywork, crash helmets and various artefacts would raise tidy sums from an audience clearly not hindered by problems with their bank managers.

The team had done well to escape from Alcatraz to the relative freedom of the pit lane

Paul played his part by bidding for a signed set of Barrichello's flameproof overalls, prompting the auctioneer's dry observation that the fledgeling team was looking after its budget since they seemed to need the overalls for the Grand Prix. Paul would have the last laugh. By Sunday evening, the value of that particular item would have risen considerably.

But first Rubens had to pass the equally stiff test of earning a decent place on the starting grid. Qualifying would mean just as much as a race in which overtaking, because of the tight nature of the track, would be a luxury.

Saturday proved to be another examination of the team's ability to adapt quickly in the face of the unexpected. Tests with the car in race trim proved satisfactory when tried first thing in the morning session, but when the car was adapted to suit the demands of a fast lap during qualifying it did not feel as good.

'Both drivers had the beginnings of a problem caused by the new set-up we were trying,' said Jenkins. 'So we decided not to go that way during qualifying. But that meant that both drivers went into qualifying with different set-ups from the ones they ran in the morning.'

Guesswork was involved to a certain degree but Barrichello found that the car was much better than before. He finished a hectic qualifying session in tenth place – and was disappointed to be that far back.

'The times on the grid are really close,' he said. 'You can see it would have taken just another two-tenths of a second to put me in the top six. But overall, I'm pleased with the way everything has worked out. The successful changes show how well the team is working. They are thinking big, finding solutions.'

Magnussen had lost time in the morning while a loose steering rack was attended to, and had one of his qualifying runs spoiled when he came across debris caused by Verstappen crashing his Tyrrell. Magnussen may have qualified in nineteenth place but at least he had brought his car back in one piece. The problem with Monaco was that any incident was usually severely punished, several teams having major repair work on their hands. Preparations that night in the Stewart-Ford corner of the car park would be routine.

Meanwhile, down by the Ford motorhome, Di and Stuart Spires were laying out a long table to receive Stewart's guests for a three-course dinner, preferable to running the gauntlet of the local restaurants on race weekend. Stewart Grand Prix were entertaining top-ranking personnel from HSBC,

Guesswork was involved to a certain degree but Barrichello found that the car was much better than before

Texaco, the Malaysian Government, Ford and Hewlett-Packard. With insufficient passes available to bring everyone onto the trackside during the day, this was the perfect answer.

Besides, most guests were happy to watch the action from the balcony of a rented apartment overlooking the first corner, given the clutter of the paddock and the pit lane when at full working strength. And the very important visitors would join Jackie and Helen and other team principals for dinner in the palace as guests of HSH Prince Rainier. In a place awash with money no amount of cash could buy an invitation that significant. It was even beyond the powerful influence of Bernie Ecclestone, the head of Formula One. Which perhaps went some way towards explaining the location of the Stewart motorhome. In any case, that was now an irrelevance. It was the race that mattered most.

The perfect conditions of the previous three days gave way to dark clouds about an hour before the Grand Prix was due to start. Reading the conditions correctly and setting up the cars accordingly would influence the result just as much the skill of the driver and the advanced technology incorporated in his car.

Ever since the team's involvement in Formula One, Dave Stubbs had received words of advice from Dickie Stanford, formerly a mechanic during Stubbs' time at Williams but now the team manager. They met in the paddock briefly and Stubbs asked Stanford what he knew about the weather prospects. Stanford said his best information was that there would be a few spots of rain, but nothing much to worry about. Stubbs glanced at the threatening sky and wondered if his friend was winding him up. Half an hour later, shortly before the cars were due to go to the starting grid, Stubbs checked again – and the answer was the same.

'He said it was going to rain quite heavily about half an hour before the start, but not for long, and not enough to make it a wet race,' said Stubbs. 'We went onto the grid and that's exactly what happened. So I thought, "Maybe they've got it right." Then it started to really come down and I thought, "Mmm . . . maybe not." Even if it did stop raining, there was no way you could start with slicks.'

It was with some surprise therefore that rivals watched the Williams mechanics remove the tyre blankets to reveal slick tyres on the cars of Frentzen and Villeneuve occupying first and third places on the grid. This was taking

In a place awash with money no amount of cash could buy an invitation that significant the word of their weather forecaster too far. The rest, the Stewart drivers included, chose grooved wet tyres. Straightaway, Barrichello knew that the Williams drivers would not be a factor – provided he could find a way past without becoming involved in the bumping and boring which was bound to ensue on such a narrow circuit. The first lap would be crucial.

As the field waited under the dripping palm trees on Boulevard Albert 1er, Barrichello checked his immediate surroundings. Ahead were Jean Alesi and Mika Hakkinen, two hard-charging drivers to be avoided on a good day, never mind one as perilous as this. As the red lights went out, Barrichello found the perfect balance between throttle and clutch and passed the Benetton and McLaren without a problem. Using the right amount of caution, but taking advantage of the moment, he ducked past Herbert's Sauber, Coulthard's McLaren and the slithering Villeneuve. At the end of the first lap the Stewart-Ford was fifth. It had to rank as one of the best first laps by any driver during the season.

By the end of the second lap, Barrichello had found a way past Frentzen. After five laps he was third, having taken advantage of a mistake by Ralf Schumacher. Barrichello was perfectly placed, but the objective now was to keep his head while those around him were losing theirs.

There were extraordinary scenes as damaged cars littered the circuit. Coulthard had lost control of his McLaren when braking for the harbour chicane, a mistake which triggered a series of shunts, one of which involved his team-mate. Hakkinen piled into the back of Alesi, sending the Benetton across the kerb and into the path of Irvine, who took avoiding action and was hit from behind by Hill, the Arrows suffering terminal damage while the Ferrari was able to continue. Barrichello was ahead of this chaos and Magnussen was fortunate to find a way through and settle into ninth place at the end of lap ten – by which time Rubens was second, and going strong. It was almost too much for the team to take in.

There were rapid calculations going on as fuel-consumption rates – in need of revision because of the slower pace and the absence of sustained maximum revs – were worked out. There was also the question of the weather. If the rain stopped then Barrichello would be coming in at some point for slick tyres. Fuel would be added at the same time. But how much?

As the race moved into the second quarter there was no sign of the skies clearing. Maybe Rubens could go non-stop since the chances were that the

Barrichello was perfectly placed, but the objective now was to keep his head while those around him were losing theirs

distance run would be less than scheduled if the race was stopped (as required by the regulations) at the two-hour maximum. Meanwhile, the Williams drivers had long since given up the unequal struggle and stopped for wet tyres, their race completely wrecked.

Not so the Stewart-Ford team. Michael Schumacher may have been in a league of his own at the front but Barrichello, half a minute behind the Ferrari, was lapping just as quickly. No one else in the field could match them for pace, the Bridgestones on the Stewart-Ford clearly working very well as Rubens gradually pulled away from Fisichella's Jordan in third place.

As the one-hour mark approached, the weather eased and the lap times reduced by a couple of seconds. Schumacher made a planned pit stop at the end of lap thirty-two but his 41-second advantage allowed him to rejoin without losing the lead. Now the gap between the Ferrari and the Stewart was down to 18 seconds. This was a crucial moment. Should Rubens carry on? Or would he need to come in for fuel? It was touch and go. Calculations suggested he might just make it without stopping.

The question was answered when the rain intensified and Schumacher began to pull away by two seconds a lap. At the same moment, Barrichello came on the radio and said he thought the tyres were going off slightly. With more than half a minute in hand over third place, it was sensible to bring him in for a splash of fuel and a fresh set of wet tyres. This was duly done at the end of lap thirty-nine, and the stop was executed perfectly. Schumacher spent 28.054 seconds in the pit lane; Barrichello, 28.192 seconds. The Stewart team were clearly up to scratch in that department too.

There was now a minute separating the leaders, with Barrichello a similar distance ahead of Irvine's Ferrari in third place. And the rain continued to fall. If anything, it was heavier than before, the track now a treacherous skating rink requiring delicate control as the survivors – half the field had retired – aimed for a finish.

Magnussen had been doing an unobtrusive but excellent job. On lap thirty-eight there were two Stewart-Fords in the first six as Jan overtook the inconsistent Fisichella. Magnussen was lapping close to Barrichello's pace and closing the gap on the fifth-place Tyrrell of Mika Salo. At the end of lap forty-four Jan was instructed to make his pit stop. That went according to plan (28.580 seconds in the pit lane). Unfortunately, he was back in the pits again at the end of the very next lap.

It was touch and go. Calculations suggested he might just make it without stopping

'It had been a difficult race,' Jan recalled later. 'The weather kept changing; sometimes it rained a lot, sometimes a little. It would change from lap to lap. After my pit stop, coming out of the tunnel, braking down into the chicane, the tyres were new, I locked up and went straight across the chicane and took the front wing off.'

It cost more than half a minute to stop for a replacement, Magnussen rejoining in seventh place, which he held until the end. Meanwhile, with about half an hour remaining, this race was far from over. The telemetry in the Stewart-Ford pit was indicating that all was far from well with Barrichello's engine, a hydraulic leak possibly jeopardizing all that good work. There was nothing for it but to cross their fingers and hope.

On lap fifty-three Schumacher disappeared into an escape road after locking his brakes. He emerged with his car still intact. There were mixed feelings in the Stewart camp. The Ferrari driver had totally dominated this race and a last-minute victory for Stewart would be tainted by that thought. Second place would do fine, thank you very much.

It seemed there would be time for two more laps. Would Barrichello make it?

The clock ticked ever so slowly. Lap fifty-five. Only twelve minutes remaining. Second place – six championship points! Keep going, Rubens! Keep going! The Stewart-Ford was under no threat from anyone or anything other than the vagaries of the machinery. The telemetry continued to receive worrying messages from the car. But the SF-1 was still running. As the two-hour mark approached and Schumacher completed his sixty-first lap, it seemed there would be time for two more laps. Would Barrichello make it?

Jackie and Paul crouched over the television and computer monitors positioned behind the pit wall. They were beneath trees on what, for 362 days of the year, is a traffic island in the middle of the promenade. Right now, this was the centre of the universe. They hardly spoke. Nothing else mattered beyond the blurred images on those television monitors. Two more laps. Second place at Monaco. Surely they were not about to be robbed at the eleventh hour?

The television showed that Schumacher was lapping very slowly. With more than a minute in hand over Barrichello, he could afford to. Michael was trying avoid having to complete another lap. If he reached the finish line any time after the two hours were up, then that would be it. Race over. The Stewart-Ford team quietly thanked him. They did not need the drama of another 2.09 miles. Irvine and Panis were on the same lap as Barrichello.

If Rubens failed to go the extra mile, he would be fourth. Not bad. But not second. At Monaco.

The television focused on the red Ferrari as it slithered gently out of the final corner, the digital stopwatch at the bottom of the screen registering 2hrs 00m 01s. The race was over. All Barrichello had to do was reach the flag.

Now the wait. Rubens had been 63 seconds behind as he crossed the line at the beginning of the last lap. There as a brief lull and then a white car appeared. It was Salo's Tyrrell, one lap down in fifth place. Then his team-mate, Verstappen, two laps behind in eighth place. Fisichella's yellow Jordan appeared, a disappointing sixth.

Where's Rubens? He should be here by now. The telemetry continued to show that the car was still running. Berger's Benetton splashed down the main straight, two laps behind in ninth place, a mere bit player on this dramatic stage.

The television cameras now had Barrichello in view. Onto the pit straight for the final time. Five hundred metres along the gently curving road and simultaneously coming into view, a sea of white-overalled arms waving furiously from the Stewart pit and, not far beyond them, the man with the chequered flag. As the travel-stained car rushed past, pandemonium broke out in the centre of the universe.

The release of tension manifested itself in hugs, tears and a huge wave of euphoria. Second place! Six points! At Monaco! Only the team's fifth race! And there, for good measure, was Magnussen coming home seventh. Brilliant! For a couple of seconds, no one quite knew what to do next.

Attention turned to the Royal Box, handily placed for Stewart a few metres to the right, on the opposite side of the track. Already, the gendarmes and officials had formed a cordon into which would be allowed the first three cars. And no one else. This would, in effect, be a temporary parc ferme before the cars would be removed to the parc ferme proper for checking by officials and final release to the teams. Under no circumstances were team-members allowed to enter parc ferme unless instructed. In his understandable delight and anxiety to congratulate his driver, Paul Stewart burst through the cordon. Dave Stubbs, watching from the pit wall and well versed in the rules, almost had heart failure. If the officials decided to, they could throw the book at Stewart-Ford. And who could tell what that might mean. Fortunately, in all the excitement, the moment passed without comment.

**Second place!
Six points! At Monaco!
Only the team's
fifth race!**

Jackie watched Rubens climb the six red-carpeted steps to the podium and shake hands with Prince Rainier. Four times – five, if you include his victory in the Monaco Formula Junior race in 1964 – Stewart had enjoyed that privilege. And now there would be a sixth. After the cups had been presented and the anthems played, Jackie turned to walk away. François Mazet, a member of the Monaco organizing team, tapped Stewart on the shoulder and said Prince Rainier wished to offer his congratulations. It was twenty-four years since Jackie had climbed those steps. He never felt more proud than he did at that moment, the family feeling evident within the team being emphasized when Paul was asked to join his father.

The entire team floated on air as they packed up their soaked belongings in the pit lane. Rubens, meanwhile, was whisked away to the media centre, where he was instantly besieged by Brazilian reporters.

'This is a really great moment for me,' he grinned. 'It's a new team, we've done so little testing, we've had our problems – but today makes up for it all. It was hard to overtake at the start, but the only other problem was keeping my concentration in the final minutes.

'Coming to this team has been the chance of my life. As the race came to an end, I kept saying, "Please, give me the chance to finish." I was thinking that I have been with Stewart since November, and I have seen how hard everyone has worked: all that was going through my mind. Maybe that's why I made a mistake and went straight on at the chicane! After that, my car was touching [the ground] a little but I checked on the gap to the car behind me and saw it was steady, so I decided to keep going.

'I'm not even going to think about the future yet. It's just great to be here, on the podium at Monaco. It's not so long ago that I used to get up at eight in Brazil and watch Senna at Monaco. For me to be on the podium here is something else.'

The celebrations shifted to the Ford motorhome, where rain lashing on the awning failed to drown the popping of champagne corks and a positive roar of animated conversation among the guests and team-members standing shoulder to shoulder. Jackie and Paul were interviewed incessantly and neither minded repeating a wonderful theme.

'I've never been happier in my whole career: not from a victory, not from a championship, never!' exclaimed Jackie, still clutching the silver cup. 'I've never been emotional about my racing either but Paul and I sat together

'I've never been happier in my whole career: not from a victory, not from a championship, never!' exclaimed Jackie

throughout the race, and when Rubens crossed the line, we both burst out crying. I'm happy, I'm relieved, I'm pleased, I'm thankful. Rubens and Jan did a wonderful job, Ford really delivered, both with reliability and driveability, and as for Bridgestone – well, it's their first year in Formula One, it's our first year in Formula One, and with them as with all our partners, there is a synergy which is really developing. It's fantastic for us to be able to deliver for all of them.

'But more than that, Monaco is the jewel in the Formula One crown. I have never been second here before – and, but for a certain Mr Schumacher, Ferrari would have been second today . . . '

That was a fair point but one which the team-members were not about to dwell on, thankful as they were to have taken second place and establish a place on the points table. Stubbs, Le Fleming, Jenkins and Malcolm Tierney (Magnussen's engineer) stopped by and took a few moments to enjoy a drop of champagne and reflect on their achievement. Glass in hand, Jenkins was as thoughtful as ever.

'This race,' he said quietly, 'is not a technical event, it's not about roll bars and details like that. This is a people event, and a result like today's is a marvellous fillip for all of them. And I'm glad for all these guys' – pointing to Redding, Le Fleming and Tierney – 'because they gave up jobs with other teams to come here.

'Stewart-Ford is still a small enough team for everyone in it to be flat out most of the time: just as the race team put in the hours at the tracks, so the people at the factory work tremendous hours to play their part. This is their day as much as anyone's.'

It was a point well made on a day when it was easy to get carried away. The season had barely started. At that very moment, up in the dingy multi-storey car park as the mechanics peeled off their soaked flameproof overalls, preparations were already in hand for the next race.

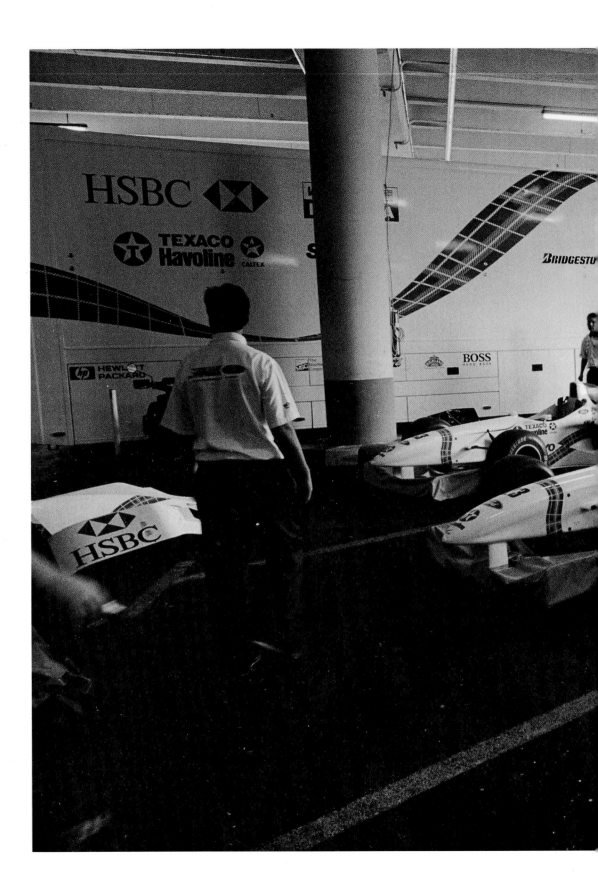

Unromantic, but it's home. The team spread themselves out in the multi-storey car park at Monaco.

ABOVE. Mind your toes.
The cramped pit lane.
RIGHT. Marshals play a vital
role at Monaco.

LEFT. Le Fleming, Barrichello and Stewart keep an eye on the opposition's lap times during qualifying. BELOW. Rubens splashes through the swimming-pool chicane on his way to a brilliant second place.

ABOVE. Mr Hiroshi Yasukawa, the head of Bridgestone, doesn't seem to know where to put himself in the Stewart pit.

LEFT. Sponsors' haven. A view from an apartment overlooking the first corner and the magnificent harbour beyond.

ABOVE. He's done it! The moment of realization that second place is sealed as the Stewarts watch the television monitor.

RIGHT. Sheer delight as Rubens joins Paul and Jackie in the paddock.

BELOW. Rubens gets his reward from his wife, Silvana.

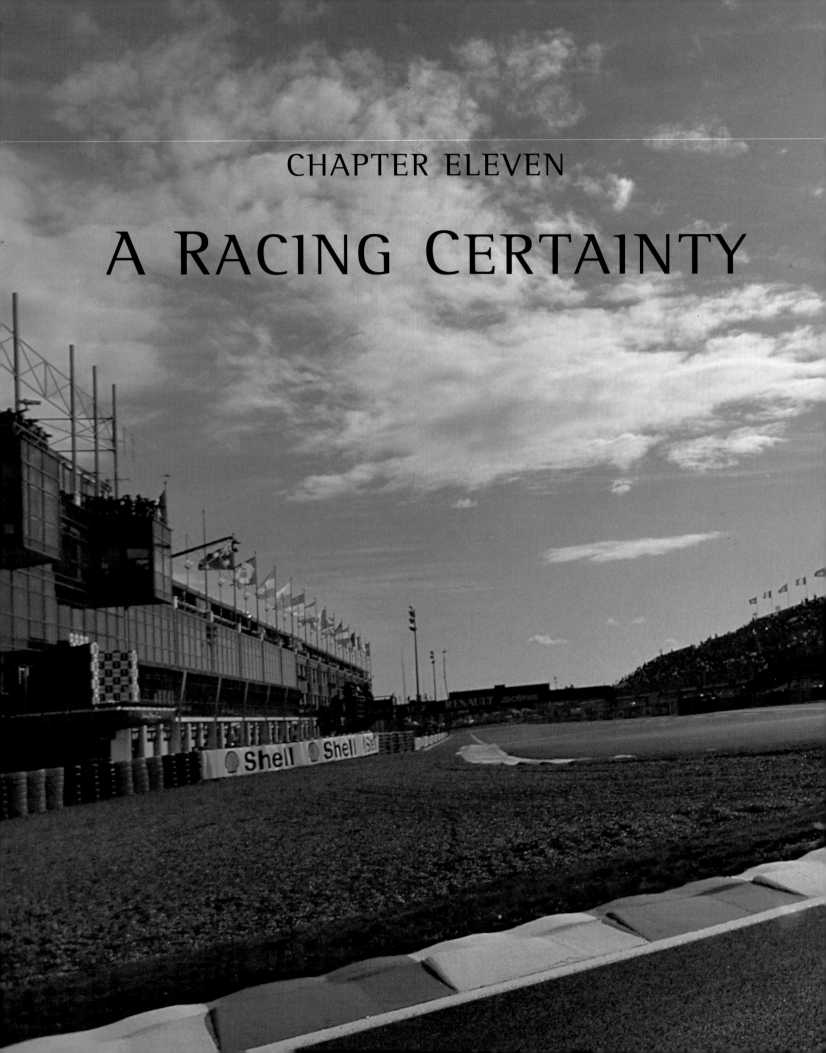

CHAPTER ELEVEN

A RACING CERTAINTY

THE STEWART-FORDS were seventeenth and twenty-second fastest in Spain, the team's worst qualifying performance of the season. It was a blunt reminder that Grand Prix racing is an on-going business. Monaco was history.

In fact, the euphoria was brief. A two-day test had been scheduled for the following Tuesday and Wednesday at Magny-Cours in France. There was no time for relaxing on the Sunday night at Monaco as the mechanics stripped down the cars, changed engines and gearboxes and packed the trucks. They finished at 1.30 a.m. By 8.00 a.m. they were on the road for the seven-hour drive into the centre of France. Then it took several more hours to unload and set up in readiness for the test session the following day. They finished at 1.00 a.m. So much for celebrating second place.

In fact, there was a timely moment of self-congratulation a few days later as everyone gathered at the headquarters in Milton Keynes. Rubens and Paul addressed the workforce from the factory floor. Rubens thanked everyone for their efforts and inscribed a bottle of Moët et Chandon. Barrichello wrote: *To the best team, my best memories, my best regards and my best champagne.* The atmosphere inside that hive of industry, momentarily at rest, had never been more positive.

'To see the look on people's faces as he spoke about his pride in his Monaco performance was a reminder of why we all do this,' said Alan Jenkins.

Seven days later, Jenkins received a reminder of just how capricious the sport could be. Much had been expected of the team's performance in Barcelona. This, after all, was the first time they were visiting a track on which the engineers had accumulated data thanks to the test session the previous February. The test at Magny-Cours had been successful and there was every reason to believe the Monaco momentum would continue in Spain. Now this. The ninth and eleventh rows of the grid and no obvious reason why. Both drivers had been pleased with the balance of their cars. Yet the lap times were not there.

The race was not much better. There was a milestone of sorts when Magnussen, running a lonely race in thirteenth place, gave the team their first full-distance finish in normal conditions (as opposed to the Monaco race which had been shortened in length and run in the wet). The oil-system problems evident in previous races appeared to have been cured but more worrying was the major engine failure which had sidelined Barrichello while holding an uninspiring eleventh place just after half distance.

More telling, too, was the Brazilian's reference to an absence of straight-line speed when it came to vain attempts at overtaking. For the first time, in

Seven days later, Jenkins received a reminder of just how capricious the sport could be

public at least, Stewart's unease with the performance of the Ford Zetec-R V10 engine was beginning to surface. By the time the team had moved on to the seventh round of the championship in Canada, the subject was being raised by the media. Jackie, attending a press briefing in Montreal, was asked outright for his opinion. This, after all, was on territory not far from Ford's world head-quarters in Michigan. And, ironically, this was the very race where, two years before, the germ of the Stewart-Ford team had been planted.

'You have to remember,' said Stewart, 'this is a five-year programme. Renault, Peugeot and Mercedes-Benz took a long time to make their engines become reliable and competitive enough to do the job those teams wanted. The Ford Zetec-R V10 is only two years old. We're hopeful we will have more performance by the British Grand Prix and another increase later in the season. I can assure you that Ford are taking this very, very seriously. I have had a relationship with Ford and Cosworth which goes back almost thirty-three years. They have won more races than any other manufacturer and you can be sure they are not in it to be seen as failures.'

That was the public relations speak. The next morning, Stewart would have a more intense conversation with Jac Nasser as he spoke for thirty minutes on the telephone with the President of Ford. It was no coincidence either that Neil Ressler and Bob Rewey, two of the Ford executives behind the Formula One project, would be arriving in Montreal on the Saturday. It would be a timely appearance in more ways than one.

Both cars were running the latest Project 6 engines for qualifying. Barrichello had been making reasonable progress – tenth fastest on Friday, sixth fastest on Saturday morning – and it was decided to take a gamble and run the car with very little downforce: in other words, sacrifice handling in the corners for speed on the straight.

The plan worked. On his very last run during qualifying, Barrichello stunned everyone with third fastest time, less than three-tenths of a second off Villeneuve's pole position. Another milestone for Stewart-Ford, one which was just as impressive as Monaco and made rivals take serious note. In fact, the experience was so new and unexpected that it took a couple of minutes to dawn on Stuart Sykes that he would need to hustle Rubens to the media centre for the mandatory press conference for the fastest three drivers. Then Sykes returned to the garage collect quotes for the daily press release.

'We are extremely pleased with what I must honestly admit is an unex-pectedly good qualifying position,' said Paul Stewart. 'It's due to a combina-

On his very last run during qualifying, Barrichello stunned everyone with third fastest time

tion of things: the work leading up to the race that Ford and Cosworth have been doing on the engine side, and our development work on the chassis and more aerodynamic development carried out by Eghbal Hamidy.'

The lesson from Barrichello's performance was that the chassis and aerodynamics were working exceptionally well. And twenty-first place for Magnussen suggested that he was still having difficulty on this type of track, one which called for frequent and heavy applications of the brake pedal. With one car on the front of the grid and the other at the back, Jackie would have a long walk as he checked on both drivers just before the start of the race.

Any hopes the team may have had of a decent finish were dashed within seconds of the start. An outstanding qualifying position came to nothing when the engine bogged down, the car hesitated and, immediately, Barrichello was in eighth place as the field funnelled through the first series of corners. And that was not the end of the bad news. In the scramble – ironically caused, in part, by the slow-moving Stewart-Ford – the Prost of Olivier Panis struck the back of a McLaren, the Prost's nose section spinning into the path of Magnussen and Panis's team-mate, Shinji Nakano. The Prost and the Stewart managed to avoid the obstacle – but then collided. Magnussen posted the first retirement of the race.

Barrichello struggled to hold on to a midfield place before having to give best to the Tyrrell-Fords, an embarrassing state of affairs since Mika Salo and Jos Verstappen were running V8 Ford engines which were hardly state of the art. Barrichello's misery was ended when the gearbox refused to select sixth gear, a problem which had not arisen before. He stopped for good after thirty-five laps. This was not what anyone wanted for the return to Europe and the next round in France, followed by an important race for the team, the British Grand Prix. Despite the success in Monaco, the pressure was building again. And the stress factor would not be helped by petty difficulties along the way.

When Stewart's transporters arrived at Magny-Cours in time to unload and prepare for the French Grand Prix, they found that only two garages had been allocated to the team. Everyone else had at least three, the minimum needed for three cars and the mass of equipment to service them. The keys to the third garage, which lay vacant next door, were finally handed over on the night before practice began. No reason was given for the delay. It was not the end of the world. But it was unnecessary aggravation.

'We just can't understand the reason for that,' said Jackie. 'The garage

> Barrichello struggled to hold on to a midfield place before having to give best to the Tyrrell-Fords, an embarrassing state of affairs

wasn't being used for anything else and it was obvious that we would be unable to get three cars into the area we had been allocated. Sometimes I wonder if it's intentional; we are new boys and this is part of the initiation.'

It could also be construed as continuing petty jealousy. Attitudes had been hardened in Barcelona when Jackie appeared in the pit lane with the King of Spain. It looked to some as though Stewart was taking his natural affinity with royalty from many nations a step too far. In fact, King Juan Carlos, an acquaintance for the past twenty-five years, had called Stewart personally to arrange an unofficial visit to the track on the Friday morning. The King wished to dispense with the protocol which formalizes his every movement in public. Stewart, had he wanted to, could hardly have said no.

They travelled together in Stewart's Ford Galaxy, Jackie driving with the King in the front seat and a bunch of security men shoulder to shoulder in the back. Stewart took his guest to see Bernie Ecclestone before visiting the top teams, including Ferrari where, curiously, the team manager was nervous about allowing Stewart too close to the cars. There was only time for a brief look at Stewart Grand Prix at the end of the visit; proof, if it were needed, that this had been nothing more than an act of friendship. Naturally, some chose not to see it that way.

Whatever form any resentment may have taken, it was not going to bother Stewart unduly. He had more pressing concerns as the season reached the halfway point. The team's budget had been sufficient to get Stewart Grand Prix up and running, but now they had to progress. There was a need for a wind tunnel, new premises, a test team and so on.

'The budget we had was to go racing,' explained Stewart. 'It allowed us to use someone else's wind tunnel and to pay for it. But, really, we need our own in order to do the job properly. In fact, HSBC has enlarged their involvement with us; their name is more prominent on the sidepods and the front wings. So, thanks to their increased investment, we have more money. But our budget is far from being full enough to allow the purchase of the things we need, facilities which the top teams already have in place.'

Stewart admitted that his financial calculations were being made difficult by uncertainty over the future distribution of payments from the sport itself. Prize and television monies are handled by FOA but Stewart Grand Prix would not be entitled to any reward until they had completed at least one year and then been admitted to the inner sanctum when asked the sign the Concorde Agreement, the sport's charter. Considering the part Stewart had played in the Monaco Grand Prix – not to mention a major involvement in numerous media

It could also be construed as continuing petty jealousy

features promoting Formula One – the absence of financial reward seemed mean-minded, not to say bizarre.

'To begin with, it seemed like trying to join a secret society,' said Jackie. 'We just didn't know what the financial numbers were – actually, I'm not sure we know yet. Hopefully, next year we are going to be members of the Concorde Agreement and a substantial amount of money should come from that. That's important to us. The agreement will give us prize money and travel money as well as a share of other benefits, including television revenue. We feel we are as much a part of the TV show as everyone else but, as things stand, we are receiving less money and that stops us being competitive.'

In Formula One, back-handed compliments do not come much higher than that but it would not help the search for competitiveness in the short term as the team finally settled into their three garages at Magny-Cours.

A thoroughly wet weekend, however, might be of some assistance. The signs were good – if you could call them that – when the persistent rain, which had visited the region for most of the week, stretched into Friday's practice. Once again the Bridgestones were complementing a nicely balanced chassis, Barrichello's name being consistently near the top of the timing screen. Then the rain stopped towards the end of the final session and Rubens finished the day in tenth place. Magnussen, the recipient of yet more bad luck, had been sidelined by a misbehaving throttle which, in turn, damaged the gear ratios. 'Never mind,' he shrugged. 'It can only get better during qualifying.' This time, his optimism would be rewarded, but not before the mechanics had been hard at work during free practice on Saturday morning.

Barrichello had completed a handful of laps. As his car was pushed backwards into the garage, Andy Le Fleming, having received a message from the Cosworth engineers manning the telemetry, came on the radio and spoke quietly to his driver.

'The engine is apparently about to blow, Rubens . . . so that's it.'

It was bad news/good news again. Bad, because a graph on the telemetry screen monitoring Barrichello's engine had dipped where it shouldn't. Good, because the warning had prevented the engine from self-destructing out on the circuit. Apart from marooning the driver and his car, the mangled remains of the engine would have prevented the Cosworth engineers from gleaning vital information. At least they could now take the engine apart and establish the cause. But that did not answer the more urgent question – what to do next.

The rules prevented the use of the spare car until the start of qualifying, which was a pity because the back-up chassis was sitting there, ready to go.

'The engine is apparently about to blow, Rubens . . . so that's it.'

There would shortly be a half-hour break before the final forty-five minutes of free practice. There was much work to be done on the track considering very little had been learned in the wet on the previous day. The answer was to remove the engine from the spare car and fit it to Barrichello's race chassis. There was a fresh engine at the back of the garage but, unlike the V10 in the spare car, the new engine was not dressed and ready for action with ancillary parts such as radiators already in place. Decision made, the mechanics went to work.

There was a great deal of urgency about this task, but no hint of desperation. The emphasis was on speed and safety, each mechanic springing to his allotted task without needing to be told what to do next.

Not much was said but the mood was cheery. This sort of chore was no more than any self-respecting mechanic would expect to tackle on a normal working day at a racetrack. The fact that the Stewart-Ford boys were working with such practised skill and calm indicated that the team had long since become an efficient unit. It was a fact which was the cause of some pride to the management and Dave Redding, the chief mechanic.

'Here you feel you're shaping the team, setting things up as you think it ought to be done,' said Redding. 'There's a lot more involvement day to day than I had when working as a number one mechanic with McLaren. Before I actually started here, one of my tasks was to help identify and recruit the right people. In fact I did everything I could to make my life easier when I eventually got here!

'The core of the team is very good, as is the way the people here want to operate: high standards of cleanliness and presentation. There's a commonly held idea of how we want it to be, how things should be done. It helps if the chain of command shares that view of things.'

Sixteen minutes after Le Fleming's announcement about stopping play, the engine from the spare car was being offered against the back of Barrichello's race chassis. Thirty-five minutes later, Rubens was in the cockpit, ready to go. The effort was worthwhile. The lessons learned during that brief period on the track would translate later in the day to thirteenth on the grid, just about where the team reasonably expected to be after such a disrupted practice. Better still, Magnussen had qualified fifteenth to equal his best performance of the season so far. And there was the chance of rain on race day.

Sure enough, the track was wet at the start of the Sunday morning warm-up. Barrichello was immediately on the pace, the team operating with practised efficiency. It was noticeable how Jackie and Paul said very little.

'The core of the team is very good, as is the way the people here want to operate'

Neither did Alan Jenkins. There was no need since the programme had already been mapped out. It was left to Andy Le Fleming and Malcolm Tierney to communicate with the drivers and what Le Fleming in particular had to say sounded very good. As Barrichello flashed past the pits, plumes of spray gleaming against the white seats of the half-filled grandstand opposite, Le Fleming's voice, a tinge of excitement in the tone, said simply: 'In, Rubens. P1.'

Two minutes later and the Stewart-Ford was sounding rough as Barrichello held a thumb on the speed-restrictor button which automatically cut the engine revs in order to prevent the car from going above 120 k.p.h. in the pit lane. Then, in preparation for the pit stops in the race, Rubens pulled up inch-perfect on the white lines marked on the pit apron.

'The tyres are really good!' he enthused. His words infused the team with a fresh urgency. The good news had travelled fast, three camera crews appeared from nowhere to film the pace-setters of the moment. The car was checked over and Barrichello sent out to see what he could learn during the final fifteen minutes. The rain had stopped but, despite the drying track, Barrichello managed to finish the warm-up in third place, with Magnussen eleventh. The forecast said that the rain would not return until the final stages of the race. The hope at Stewart-Ford was that they would get that far.

They didn't. Barrichello, anxious not to have a repeat of his poor start in Canada, overcompensated by giving the engine too many revs. As the rear wheels spun he went nowhere and Magnussen was able to jump ahead of his team-mate. The white cars held midfield positions and contributed very little to the race. Then they retired within minutes of each other at half distance, Magnussen going out when a broken cooling duct led to brake trouble, Barrichello suffering a failure of the Project 6 engine in its first race. The mood as the packing-up process began was downbeat, to say the least.

In sixteen starts, the Stewart-Fords had retired thirteen times even though they had, on occasions, gone far enough to be classified as finishers. True, one of the three 'proper' finishes had been second place at Monaco, but that epic result was gradually being submerged by persistent unreliability. There was no doubt that the promise was there; the problem was, the team had been giving themselves little opportunity to show it. On the other hand, Stewart-Ford had barely been able to catch their breath since rolling out the new car just seven months before. Time had rocketed. Now it was the British Grand Prix next on the calendar. It seemed only yesterday that Jackie had been sitting in the Ford Scorpio making arrangements for his home race while en route to the very first Silverstone test of the SF-1.

The good news had travelled fast, three camera crews appeared from nowhere to film the pace-setters of the moment

'It's been never-ending,' admitted Jackie. 'Just keeping up with it all has been my biggest challenge. I think that has been one of the most unexpected things; time has passed so quickly, much faster than when I was racing. There have been occasions recently when I felt that I was not driving the bus, I was running hard just to keep up with it. There is always a fire of some kind which needs putting out and that takes time out of your overcrowded life.'

His schedule for the weekend of the British Grand Prix was a mammoth piece of work. Stewart kicked off at the circuit on Thursday morning with an appointment with James Mossop of the *Sunday Telegraph*, one of a dozen media interviews on the schedule, plus many more which would be handled off-the-cuff when time permitted. Jackie's main concern – apart from the progress of the Formula One team, of course – would be the well-being of the team's business partners and their guests in various locations.

On Friday, for example, he would visit the Stewart Grand Prix guests in the Paddock Club, before repeating the process in the Ford area of the same club and then moving on to another group of Ford VIPs in the hospitality suites overlooking Brooklands corner. After that, a switch to the outside of the circuit and a climb up the Autosport Tower to the impressive Paul Stewart Racing suite on the second floor. In between, he would be keeping an eye on the progress of the PSR teams competing in the Formula Three and Formula Vauxhall support races. His progress would be monitored by William Parry and Andy Foster as the PAs ensured that Jackie did not miss a meeting with Michael Heseltine at the SGP garage before joining HRH The Duke of Kent at the British Racing Drivers' Club (BRDC).

All of this would be on Friday and Saturday. Race day, Sunday, would be even more active as Stewart took care of a party brought to Silverstone by the Malaysian High Commissioner and consisting of the Minister of Tourism and Tan Sri Arumugam, an influential businessman who had afforded important introductions to Stewart in Kuala Lumpur. In between, Jackie would undertake the whirlwind tour of hospitality sites catering for over 1,300 guests who would be expecting great things from Stewart-Ford at this splendid and uniquely British event.

There would be down-to-earth moments, too, such as during the walkabout on Saturday morning when members of the public are allowed into the pit lane. Three Scotsmen appeared, wearing makeshift kilts and T-shirts with the legend: *F1 Shock. Rab C. Nesbitt joins SGP*, a reference to the unsavoury Scotsman portrayed on the national television series. Jackie and Paul happily

'There is always a fire of some kind which needs putting out and that takes time out of your overcrowded life'

posed for photographs with the mischievous group. Then, as the pit lane was being cleared, Stewart noticed someone in a wheelchair stuck on the edge of the gathering outside the Stewart garage. He went across, signed autographs and had pictures taken. It was a simple action with a deep meaning for the man in the wheelchair.

The garage made an impressive sight with a special raised platform cordoned off to one side in order to accommodate visiting VIPs without causing discomfort for the guests and a hindrance to the team. It was typical of the attention to detail, something which had been remarked upon the previous evening. George Harrison, taking part in a motor racing chat show on BBC Radio 5 Live, had been commenting on the Stewart team before going on air.

'When I heard that Jackie was starting his own Grand Prix team,' said Harrison, 'I was excited because, as with Alain Prost and his team, I like to see former drivers involved. They know better than anyone what it's about. And they're also under no illusions about how difficult motor racing can be.

'I went to the Australian Grand Prix in Melbourne and I was very impressed with the Stewart team. They seemed to be well coordinated and under control. The car looked really good and well turned out – which was more than could be said for one or two of their rivals! Their cars looked terrible and the team-members seemed to be like a bunch of orphans with nobody talking to each other. That was not the case at Stewart. It was no surprise because Jackie is always very thorough in everything he does.

'I got to know Jackie very well in the mid-seventies. I have always been a fan of Formula One ever since I went to the British Grand Prix when it came to Aintree in 1955 and the Mercedes-Benz team had a clean sweep. So it was quite a thrill for me to meet someone like Jackie because of what he had done on the racetrack. I was not disappointed. I've since spent a lot of time with him and found that he has a good sense of humour. He's also meticulous with his business and that's reflected in the team.

'I got to know Paul when he was little. He and his brother Mark would come by my house quite a lot when they were in England and sometimes stay. I think Paul is a really nice guy. I heard someone in Melbourne say that if there were more people in the pit lane like Paul Stewart, then it would be a much nicer place. And I think that's true.

'I know you've got to be tough in Formula One but that doesn't mean to say you've got to be bad-mannered and totally ruthless. Paul is quite young in such a heavyweight business but I'm impressed with what he has managed to do.

The garage made an impressive sight with a special raised platform cordoned off to one side in order to accommodate visiting VIPs

'I thought the result in Monaco was fantastic. Particularly in the team's first year. I think that said a lot in such a difficult sport. In fact, I sometimes think it's a crazy business and I'm glad I just a spectator!'

The temporary partitions in the Silverstone garage, apart from showing sponsors' logos as usual, proudly carried the insignia of the British Racing Drivers' Club: a discreet sign of Stewart's pride in his racing heritage. But also another reminder of the pressure on the team to do well at home.

No one was feeling that pressure more than the engineers from Cosworth. Silverstone, a few miles down the road from the company headquarters in Northampton, was effectively their abode since they had spent little time at home during the previous few weeks. Nick Hayes and his team were caught between a rock and a hard place. Stewart-Ford wanted reliability but they also wanted performance. The two did not make ideal bedfellows on a development which, as Jackie had pointed out in Canada, was only in its second year. Two of the latest Project 7 engines had been run during a test at Silverstone. One engine had covered 87 miles without a problem. The other had gone for 112 miles – and run into difficulties. The Cosworth engineers had taken steps they hoped would rectify the problem while, at the same time, continuing the search for more power.

The P7 engine marked a major step forward. More than half of the components had been altered, making this the biggest change since the engine had been introduced. Modifications on such a grand scale could not be made overnight. It had taken months to complete the design and then organize the manufacture and the planning so that all of the various pieces – some of which would take longer to produce than others – would be completed at roughly the same time. And, while all of that was going on, production had continued with the P6 as well as advance planning and manufacture for the next stages on the P8 and the P9.

For the moment, however, a massive effort had gone into building enough P7 engines to see the team through the Silverstone weekend. That had entailed a three-shift system at Cosworth as the company worked round the clock. It was therefore galling to read suggestions in the press that Ford and Cosworth were not trying hard enough. It was even more painful when two of the P7s failed during practice and qualifying.

'We had no alternative,' said Ford's Martin Whitaker. 'We have to force ahead. We want to step up performance and this is the best way to learn quickly. You can test all you like on the bench and on the dyno until the engine is reliable, but that takes time which we haven't got. There is no substitute

Silverstone was effectively their abode since they had spent little time at home during the previous few weeks

for actually running in the car at a race meeting. It's very public and, unfortunately, this is sometimes the result.'

The effect of the 'result' was that Rubens Barrichello would start the British Grand Prix from the back row of the grid. There could not have been a more desperate sequence of events on this of all days. Both race cars had been fitted with P7 engines for Saturday, the spare car retaining a P6. Free practice had been encouraging, Rubens setting ninth fastest time during the course of twenty-six laps. If only he had completed one more lap, the embarrassment about to engulf the team might have been saved.

Barrichello had reported that the engine felt fine, a definite improvement over the P6. The readings on the telemetry indicated that all was well as the car was fired up and Rubens prepared to leave the garage to start qualifying. He got as far as the first corner – where the engine promptly failed without warning. One more lap in the morning and the problem would have occurred then. But, as Barrichello sprinted back to the pits, the team had to make do and put plan B into operation.

He got as far as the first corner – where the engine promptly failed without warning

The spare car was pressed into action. Barrichello left the pits, completed one flying lap, more or less as a warm-up, and then returned to the pits where an engine problem would cause the exhaust pipes to become unusually hot and promptly set fire to the underbody. It was a problem which had never occurred before. But it would happen now. Time for plan C.

The only alternative left was to use Magnussen's car. Jan completed three runs, the middle one producing a time which would be worth sixteenth place on the grid. On his final run, Magnussen felt the engine begin to lose power. Barrichello confirmed it when he jumped on board and the P7 blew up spectacularly before he could register a decent time.

'I hope I speak for the whole team when I say we accept the risks inherent in the aggressive engine development programme adopted by Ford and Cosworth,' said Jenkins immediately afterwards. 'The issues we face are not only related to engine development itself, but also to the correct implementation and understanding of the engine and its installation in the car. It is a poor reward for the effort put in by everybody, from the Cosworth engineers to the team engineers and drivers. It is particularly galling because they follow on from a very successful operation for readjustment and tuning of the chassis to meet the changing track conditions, which had left us quite optimistic. We really had made good progress.'

Jackie, meanwhile, was inclined to be more forthright as he thought about his important guests. 'Never in my entire career have I seen such a train of events as I have today,' he said. 'The only thing which impressed me was the calm manner in which the team dealt with these dramas. They were impeccable. If nothing else, I was very, very proud of the way everyone coped with failure.'

There was one P7 engine left and it was a sign of the team's intent when there was a unanimous decision to race it. Magnussen would do the honours since he had been fastest in qualifying. 'No problem,' said the Dane. 'I would rather race with the P7: we are racing for a better future, not for now.'

That summed up the team's philosophy perfectly. The only hope was that the hundreds of team guests ranged round the circuit on Sunday afternoon would understand that as both cars retired yet again.

Jackie had been with an influential group in the PSR suite in the Autosport Tower. He was able to explain events on the track, a job which gave him little pleasure. His next task was to ensure that it did not happen again. Starting now. As soon as the Stewart-Fords had retired, a scooter whisked Stewart to the helicopter pad for a trip to Battersea and then on by car to Heathrow in time to catch Concorde to New York. A thirty-minute connection had him on a commuter plane to Detroit. By the time he reached the Ritz Carlton, the weekend's events had caught up and he retired, exhausted, at 9 p.m. local time. Refreshed, Jackie was ready at 6 a.m for a busy week at the Ford headquarters as he carried out vehicle testing and assessment during the day and had meetings and dinners with Jac Nasser and senior management each night. There were no prizes for guessing the subject at the top of Stewart's agenda.

'We said we could be in contention in five years,' said Stewart. 'The only way we can achieve our goal is by that level of management being aware of the good news and the bad news. We can identify good chassis performance and good aerodynamics. The engine issue is our biggest concern. But, as far as I am concerned, Silverstone is history. This is the start of another week.'

Indeed so. One race did not make a summer. The wonder was that the Stewart-Ford team had achieved so much in the seven months since the SF-1 had ventured down the runaway at Boreham. The conception and birth had been difficult enough. The growth had brought its own agonies but, as with any upbringing involving sweat and worry, the moments of pleasure had been without equal. The new Grand Prix team had arrived. Regardless of the trials and tribulations, Racing Stewart was a racing certainty.

ABOVE. Under scrutiny. Every movement and function on each car is monitored on the telemetry screens at the back of the garage.

RIGHT. What now? There's much to discuss at the technical debrief after a disappointing qualifying session.

RIGHT. Royal connection. Jackie guides his old friend King Juan Carlos around the garage in Barcelona. BELOW. Solitary confinement. Magnussen reflects on his position at the back of the grid.

LEFT. Get ready. The mechanics prepare for a pit stop.

BELOW. Go! Magnussen blasts off with fresh tyres and a tank full of fuel.

ABOVE. When the talking stops. Crew members wait while the drivers do their bit on the track. RIGHT. Darren Nicholls removes the under-body prior to an engine change – one of many – in France.

ABOVE. I've seen better. Magnussen examines lap times on the monitor.
LEFT. The French show their colours at Magny-Cours.

All in a row.
The Stewart-Fords,
line astern on the
grid in France.

LEFT. Jackie is startled by the size of the audience outside the garage during the pit lane walkabout at Silverstone.

ABOVE. A Celtic interlude in the pit lane.

BELOW. Planning in progress as the marketing and public relations team hold a morning briefing outside the motorhome.

ABOVE. Briefing Cellnet guests. RIGHT. Next! Jackie emerges from the hospitality suite as Andy Foster revs the scooter, ready to visit the next port of call.

LEFT. Musical interlude.
Simon Le Bon visits the
garage during practice.
BELOW. Familiar routine.
A worthy gamble to run
the latest Ford V10 at
Silverstone resulted in
a number of engine
changes.

ABOVE. You've got to laugh. Paul keeps the mood light as Rubens contemplates starting from the back of the grid.

RIGHT. Magnussen prepares to give it his best shot as final preparations are made on the grid.

BELOW. Going nowhere. The Stewart-Fords were destined to retire.

ACKNOWLEDGEMENTS

JACKIE STEWART

This book would never have been written had it not been for the immense support and confidence provided by individuals and companies that invested in a 'future' called Stewart Grand Prix.

Paul as Managing Director and I as Chairman would never have entered Grand Prix racing without an association with a major car maker for the supply of our racing engines. I have been under contract to Ford for thirty-three years – they were the natural partner for this new endeavour.

Ford took a big gamble in entrusting to an untried new team the company's proud heritage in Formula One. Without the confidence of Jacques Nasser, Bob Rewey, Neil Ressler, Bob Transu, Dan Rivard (now retired) and Martin Whitaker, this team would never have come together.

Since the original commitment, after a series of meetings, more people within this enormous company have become involved, providing expertise and giving their support. Ford took the almost unmatched decision to commit to a brand-new team, for a five-year programme, to provide us with the exclusive use of the factory Ford Formula One Grand Prix engine.

From there, Stewart Grand Prix had an immensely strong foundation on which to build, to select a prestigious group of sponsor partners who, I believe, are unmatched in the history of Formula One for any new team.

The Government of Malaysia, under the direct leadership of Prime Minister Mahathir, was yet another feather in our cap. As discussions progressed, Deputy Prime Minister Anwar and the Minister of Culture, Arts and Tourism, also stood behind this programme.

To have a nation whose performance has been the envy of the world and whose technology has accelerated with such success be part of our team was for us tremendously satisfying.

For Malaysia to make a commitment of this kind was immensely flattering, as well as providing an excellent example to other governments around the world. Prime Minister Mahathir had the vision of recognizing that Malaysia would be projected around the world in an exciting, glamorous, colourful and professional high-technology sport.

Without the counsel and advice of Tan Sri Arumugam, a successful Malaysian, we would not have been able to achieve the kind of access that was necessary to secure our goal.

For me personally, the association that was created with HSBC was one of the most satisfying achievements commercially in the formation of the new Stewart-Ford Team. Sir William Purves is an astute and extremely highly respected chairman, well known for his Scottish dourness and determination to achieve the very best for the multinational corporation that he has led over the last eleven years.

Sir William and John Bond, the Chief Executive Officer of HSBC, along with Mary Jo Jacobi, Head of Group Public Affairs, broke new ground in persuading the Board of HSBC to make a long-term commitment to our team. They saw the benefits of not only projecting the corporate identity in the United Kingdom and in the seventy-eight countries where HSBC have offices, but also of exposing the relatively new HSBC logo on a global basis, through the immense media coverage gained by this new team both on television and in print.

The commercial ramifications that they also saw in networking, corporate hospitality and creating new incremental business have certainly influenced the financial services world to take a new look at what sport can provide.

Texaco have 40,000 dealer outlets around the world, are one of the best-known corporate names and are among the largest and most successful corporations in their industry. They had not been in Formula One Grand Prix racing for almost twenty years. Their renewed interest in the sport for corporate image and for new opportunities of creating business was the driving force behind their arrival.

Bridgestone/Firestone, the largest tyre and rubber company in the world, with extremely impressive research and development, were our choice as a tyre supplier. 1997 has been their first year, as it is ours, in Formula One. We could have gone to the already well-established and successful competitor, but many of us in our small company thought that the future with Bridgestone/ Firestone had an immense amount of promise. They have proved in the first half of the season covered by this book that their contribution to our team has already provided us with considerable benefit and advantage.

Sanyo were an ideal partner for our first year, allowing us to reach a consumer market place that only a global company of their size and reach could supply.

Without Hewlett Packard we could not possibly have achieved so much in such a short time in our Technical and Design Department. Alan Jenkins, our Technical Director, along with Hewlett Packard, EDS and Unigraphics, created the first computer-designed Formula One car. Their technical support, and the enthusiasm of Alex Sozonoff and Joel Birnbaum, under the direction of their Chairman Lew Platt and Jim Duncan of Unigraphics, certainly eased the way and permitted us to create a Formula One car in nine months and nine days.

There are many more people and companies without whom this team could not possibly have come together. As in everything in life, it was people who in the end allowed this brand-new team of very special individuals to come together to take on a well-established, highly competitive field in the world's most high-technology sport.

As Chairman of Stewart Grand Prix, I know that my son Paul and I will be for ever grateful for the confidence, trust and assistance extended to us by all of the above – and many more besides.

MAURICE HAMILTON

This book would not have been possible without the support and help of everyone at Stewart Grand Prix. The impetus came from paul and Jackie, for whom nothing was too much trouble, and I am deeply grateful for that. Thanks are also due to Rob Armstrong, Jane Brady, Jim Brett, Hugh Hunston, Susan Johnston, Andy Le Fleming, Andy Foster, Alan Maybin, Judith McMahon, Andy Miller, William Parry and Dave Redding. In particular, I must make special mention of Nick Hayes, Alan Jenkins, David Stubbs and Stuart Sykes for their time and patience: any mistakes are mine, not theirs.

JON NICHOLSON

I would like to thank Olympus Cameras and Metro Photographic for their assistance, as well as everyone at Stewart Grand Prix who helped.

STEWART GRAND PRIX

Simon Adams, Jean Albrecht, Jay Allen, Dave Amey, Steve Armitage, Rob Armstrong, John Bailey, Rubens Barrichello, Greg Beard, Ray Beasley, Phil Bennett, Nigel Betts, Iain Bomphrey, Andy Bosworth, Shaun Bosworth, Christophe Bouqueniaux, David Boys, Jane Brady, David Brown, Michael Brudenhall, Anthony Burrows, Graham Civil, Perry Cohn, Clare Cooper, Allison Couper, Michael Courcoux, Clive Crewe, Iain Cunningham, Neil Dickie, John Digby, Rob Dorney, Paul Drewery, Andrew Duggan, Debbie Evans, Anthony Fletcher, Pete Ford, Andrew Foster, Caroline Goodacre, Kevin Gowling, Cheryl Hall, Eghbal Hamidy, Alan Harris, Jon Harriss, Neil Hayward, Andrew Henderson, Mel Henderson, Simon Herring, Christopher Hodges, Ewen Honeyman, Mike Huggins, Hugh Hunston, Su Jackson, Michael Jakeman, Kevin James, Mike Jeanes, Alan Jenkins, Susan Johnston, Anthony Jones, Heidi Kahlich, Jon Kelly, Andy Le Fleming, Philippa Leslie, Shaun Lovesey, Tim Lowcock, Sharon Lynch, Richard McAinsh, David McClurg, Colin McGrory, Craig McIlvar, Janice McIlwraith, Judith McMahon, Craig McNaughton, Jan Magnussen, Brian Magwood, Wendy Mansell, Rod Mardle, Julian Marlow, Stuart Marsh, Ellen Martin, Alan Maybin, Andy Miller, Julian Mills, Philip Millson, Simon Morley, Steve Nevey, Nigel Newton, Darren Nicholls, Simon Oakley, Ian O'Dell, Gerrard O'Reilly, Mike Overy, Hilary Palmer, Philip Parker, William Parry, Peter Phillips, Adrian Pile, David Pinches, Peter Priest, Ian Prior, Garry Puddephatt, Terry Purcell, Alan Quy, Dave Redding, Peter Reeves, Dave Rendall, Paul Reynolds, Paul Singlehurst, Jean-François Sinteff, Dave Slater, Andrew Smith, Wayne Spencer, Graham Sprowell, Jackie Stewart, Paul Stewart, David Stubbs, Clive Summers, Pete Sumner, Stuart Sykes, Toshio Tanaka, Caroline Taylor, Chris Taylor, Leon Taylor, Chris Tee, Nigel Tee, Peter Terry, Matt Thomas, Malcolm Tierney, Richard Tomlinson, Simon Turner, Glen Tyrell, Paul Warren, Malcolm Watson, Gerry Webb, Amanda Wheatcroft, Andrew Williams, Mike Williams, Nick Wiltshire.